Practical Service English

서비스 실무 영어

이원화 · 신승훈 공저

기문사
www. moonsa.co.kr

머리말 Preface

"어떻게 하면 영어를 잘할 수 있을까요" 대학강단에서 영어를 가르치기 시작하면서부터 필자가 들었던 가장 많은 질문 중 하나가 아닌가 생각한다. 현재 영어의 학습과 평가의 흐름은 단순한 문법의 암기와 이것에 대한 응용을 테스트하는 것뿐만 아니라 학생들에게 말하기, 쓰기, 읽기, 듣기에 대한 종합적인 능력을 요구하고 있다. 이러한 추세는 어쩌면 다른 나라의 언어를 배우려고 하는 사람들에게는 당연히 요구되었어야 할 것이다. '저는 말하는 영어를 하고 싶습니다', '저는 쓰기가 잘 안돼서요,' '전 말하고 듣는 건 되는데 문제만 풀면…' 학생들마다 다른 고민을 하고 다른 노력들을 해오는 것을 보면서 무엇이 학생들을 위해 가장 기본적으로 필요한 것인지에 대해 그리고 이러한 고민들을 해결할 수 있는 책을 써보겠다는 생각으로 집필에 임하였다.

여기 영어의 학습을 위한 간단한 팁 몇 가지를 전하고자 한다. 먼저 기본적인 단어와 문법에 대한 철저한 학습이다. 말은 느낌과 감정, 생각을 전달하는 것이고 이러한 것들의 정확한 전달을 위해서는 반드시 그 언어가 가지고 있는 규칙에 따라 말하고 써야만 할 것이며 이를 문법이라고 풀이할 수 있을 것 같다. 그리고 정확한 단어의 선택은 좀더 정확한 의미 전달을 위해 반드시 습득되어야 할 가장 기본적인 사항이라고 생각한다. 따라서 일정부분은 완전히 암기되어야 하고 이 부분에 대한 해결 없이 무작정 영어를 공부한다는 것은 지도 없이 사막을 벗어나는 것과 다를 바 없다고 생각한다.

둘째 우리가 배우는 것은 언어이다. 언어는 말하지 않고 듣지 않고 쓰지 않으면 결코 지식의 확장을 가져올 수 없다. 이는 현재 학생들이 좀 더 말하고 듣고 쓰는 기회를 가지고 활용하려고 노력해야 한다는 말이다.

셋째 한국에서 영어의 능력을 측정하는 시험에서의 성과를 거두기 위해서는 위에서 제시된 기본적인 문법과 단어를 완전히 익히고 어떻게 문제가 출제되는지에 대한 각 부분별 학습이 있어야 할 것이다. 여기에 좀더 세부적인 예외사항에 대해 공부하는 것만이 자신의 실력을 증명하는 하나의 중요한 방법이 될 것이다.

물론 위의 세가지 원칙 외에 많은 내용이 있을 것이다. 하지만 집을 높이 쌓기 위해 기초를 튼튼히 해야 하는 것처럼 위의 기본적인 원칙이 다른 어떠한 원칙보다 중요하다는 것을 다시 한번 강조하고 싶다.

본 교재는 또한 환대산업에 일하고자 하는 학생들이 그들의 미래 직업에 있어 친숙하게 영어를 접할 수 있도록 구성하였다. 본서의 기초 영어 회화 부분은 비스니스 회화를 기본으로 환대산업의 많은 다양한 업장에서 쓰일 수 있는 영어표현을 중심으로 구성하였다.

마지막으로 학생들의 권투를 빌며 그날이 올 때까지 매진합시다.

저자 일동

차 례 Contents

Part I

Service English

01 Greeting & Introduce

인사 및 자기소개

O·V·E·R·V·I·E·W

간단한 인사에서부터 정식적인 인사말에 관한 표현의 습득은 환대산업에서 일하려고 하는 사람들에게는 필수적인 사항이다. 상대방을 처음 만날 때는 밝은 목소리와 미소를 통해서 친근감을 표시하는 것을 잊지 말자.

Useful Expressions

Greeting

Hello! (Hi!)
How are you?
How are you doing?
How' s everything going?
How have you been?
How are you getting on?
Long time, no see
Nice to meet you.
Good morning! (afternoon, evening) My name is ~.
Welcome!

How to answer

Great!

Pretty good.

So far so good.

It couldn't be better.

Not bad.

So so.

Terrible.

And you? And yourself?

It's nice to see you.

Have a wonderful day!

See you later.

Tip

Sir/Madam의 표현은 언제 쓸까요?

현대의 영어 표현에 있어 위의 표현은 점차 줄어들고 있는 추세이다. 하지만 여전히 서비스기업, 의전행사 그리고 격식을 갖추어야 하는 곳에서는 이러한 표현들이 자주 쓰이는 편이다.

Dialogue

📖 Dialogue 1

A: Hello, My name is Jack.

B: Hi, I am Jill.

A: Nice to meet you.

B: Nice to meet you, too.

A: How are you today?

B: Pretty good!

A: It was nice to see you

B: Me too. See you later.

A: See you later.

📖 Dialogue 2

A: Welcome to Hilton hotel, how are you, Sir/ Madam?

B: Very well, thank you. And how are you?

A: Fine, thanks. What are you going to do in Seoul?

B: I'm going for shopping.

A: That sounds great.
I hope you have a nice time in Seoul.

Dialogue 3

A: How are you getting along?
B: I am keeping busy.
A: Doing what?
B: I am preparing for my interview.

Dialogue 4

A: Hello, Jack.
B: Hello, Jill. I haven't seen your for a long time.
How's everything going?
A: Nothing special. How about you?
B: Not so bad, thanks.
A: Please, say hello to your family.
B: Sure, I'll see you again.

🕮 Dialogue 5

A: Did you have a nice stay, Sir?

B: Very well, thank you.

A: When are you leaving, Sir?

B: The plane leaves at 2:00pm.

A: I see. Have you confirmed your ticket?

B: Yes, I did it a week ago.

A: Good. I hope you visit again to Seoul.

B: I hope so too. Thank you for your kindness.

A: It's my pleasure. Have a pleasant journey.

02 Requests and Responses

요청과 승낙, 감사, 거절

O·V·E·R·V·I·E·W

직장에서 뿐만 아니라 일상적인 생활에서 상대방에게 많은 부탁을 하고, 이러한 부탁에 대한 감사의 표현은 반드시 전해야 한다. 감사의 표현에 대한 응답 또한 매우 중요한 매너의 한가지이므로 반드시 익히자. 또한 많은 사람들이 거절하는 경우에 어떻게 해야 할지 잘 모르는 경우가 있다. 상대방의 기분을 상하게 하는 무리한 요구는 피하고, 정중하게 거절하는 방법을 살펴보자.

Useful Expressions

Requests

Could you do me a favor?
Can I have this?
Can you help me?
Do you mind if I move this table?
May I ask you a favour?
Would it be possible to change my reservation?
Could you tell me where is a cafeteria?
Would you possibly clean the room?
May I have your pen?

Responses

Certainly, how can I help you?

Yes, of course. Do you need any more help?

Yes, you can.

Go ahead.

That will be fine.

No problem.

That's no trouble at all.

Well, if I can.

Thanks

Thank you very much.

Thanks (a lot/a million).

Thank you for your help.

I appreciate it.

It is very kind of you to say so.

It is very kind of you.

It was a great help.

Answering

You are welcome.
Your are most welcome.
My pleasure.
Don' t mention it. That is my work.

Rejecting Someone' s your favor

I' m sorry, I am too busy now.
I' m sorry, I can' t help you.
I don' t think we can do that for you.
I' m not sure with that.
I' m afraid you may not.
Excuse me, I' ll be back right away.
Excuse me, I have something urgent.

Tip

매일 많은 사람들과 만나고 커뮤니케이션을 하는 가운데, 자신도 모르게 실수한 경우에 사과는 간단하게 Excuse me.를 사용하여 상대방의 기분을 좋아지게 할 수 있다. 만약 운전 중 접촉사고가 발생했을 때 I' m sorry.란 표현을 쓴다면 모든 잘못을 내가 인정한다는 뜻이므로 신중하게 사용해야 한다.

Dialogue

Dialogue 1

A: Could you do me a favor?

B: Yes, how can I help you?

A: Can you clean this coffee filter for me?

B: Of course.

A: Thank you so much for helping me.

B: You're welcome.

Dialogue 2

A: Could you tell me where is changing room?

B: I will show you. Come this way, please.

A: I appreciate it.

B: Don't mention it.

🕮 Dialogue 3

A: Would it be possible to change my order?

B: No, I am sorry it is too late. You should let us know at least 10minutes before.

A: I know but she changes her mind now.

B: I am sorry I can't help you. Could you put new order again?

A: Yes, I will.

B: Sorry, tell her it will take 10minutes to have food.

🕮 Dialogue 4

A: Hello, may I speak to Mr. Jun?

B: Yes, can you hold on a moment, Sir.

C: This is Mr. Jun speaking. Who's calling please?

A: Hello, this is Green. I'm calling to thank you for your dinner last week. It was wonderful and I enjoyed it very much.

C: You're welcome. I am so happy to hear that you'd enjoyed it. If there's anything that I can help you with in the future, please let me know.

A: I'll do that. Thank you again and I'll talk to you again.

🕮 Dialogue 5

A: Hello, Sir! How may I help you?
B: I think my toilet is out of order.
A: I'm so sorry for the trouble. I'll send someone up right away.
B: Yes, please.

🕮 Dialogue 6

A: Excuse me, Can I borrow your pen?
B: Yes, here it is.
A: Where can I sign?
B: You can sign below here on the registration card.
A: Oh, I see. Thanks.

🕮 Dialogue 7

A: Would you like a lunch with me today?
B: I'm afraid I can't. I have a meeting at 1 o'clock.
A: Let's make another time then.

📖 Dialogue 8

A: Did you enjoy your dinner, Sir?

B: It was great, thank you.

A: Would you like to have some more wine?

B: Yes, please.

A: Oh, I'm terribly sorry the wine is spilled out.

B: Don't worry. You spilled it on the table.

A: I will bring another glass of wine.

B: That will be great.

A: I'll be back right away.

03 Making an appointment

약속

O·V·E·R·V·I·E·W

인간관계를 유지함에 있어 많은 부분은 상대방과의 시간을 확인하고 약속을 하는 것으로 구성된다. 약속시간에 적어도 15분 전에 도착하는 것이 기본 매너이고, 또한 약속을 잡아두고도 예기치 못한 상황이 발생할 수 있으므로 이러한 즉흥적인 상황에 대비하는 자세가 필요하겠다. 따라서 공식적인 행사, 약속, 비즈니스 미팅, 캐주얼한 모임과 관련된 표현은 철저히 익히도록 하자.

Useful Expressions

Arranging your meeting

Do you have any plans for this weekend?
Do I have to work this Saturday?
Do you work this coming Sunday?
How many hours will we have before the conference?
How many covers are we expecting?
At what time can I see you?
When shall we meet?
What time will the function start?
Who is VIP this evening?
Who is coming there?

Making a plan

May I have an appointment with you this evening?
When is our appointment time with executive chef? I have a plan with my friend.
I will promise I will do your favor for the next time.
Did you check your appointment time with human resource manger?
Any time this afternoon will be OK.
I'll be free at 8 this evening.
I'm afraid I can't make it this weekend.
I'm sorry, I'm expecting someone this evening.

About your meeting

How long the meeting will be last?
When is the meeting tomorrow?
What will we discuss tonight?
Do you know why they call us?
Do we have to attend the meeting this morning?
Did you check the time of the meeting?
Are you going to have a meeting tonight?
I'm afraid I can't manage it.

Tip

서양 사람들은 자신의 이름을 걸고 약속 시간을 엄수하고 있지만, 한국 사람들은 Korean Time이란 말이 생겼을 정도로 약속 시간에 대해 엄격히 지키고 있지 않다. 나 하나쯤이란 마음가짐은 글로벌 시대를 살아가는 현대인의 매너를 흩트리는 것이며 자신의 이미지를 나쁘게 만드는 중요한 요소이다. 서양에서는 작은 모임까지도 3주 전에 미리 예약을 하거나, 참석 여부에 대해 초대자에게 반드시 답변을 보내는 배려를 잊지 않고 있다.

Dialogue

Dialogue 1

A: How many hours do we have before the conference?

B: We only have 2 more hours.

A: Guys, we need to hurry up!

B: I will finish my duty first, then help Jacky.
I think I need only 20minutes for setting up, and help them later.

A: Ok! Let move on fast. The conference will be start very soon.

🕮 Dialogue 2

A: Did you check time schedule?
B: Not yet. How's it?
A: Yes, I've just found that I have to work this Saturday.
B: Sorry to hear that. I had better check it.
A: I think we are going to be very busy this coming Saturday.
B: We should be ready for it.

🕮 Dialogue 3

A: What will we discuss this morning?
B: I heard that we need to set a plan for tomorrow function.
A: That is not necessary. I heard that the function was cancelled.
B: No, apparently there is new conference coming on.
A: Gee, we will have three different functions tomorrow.
B: I think a busy day is better than a quiet day.
A: I think so too, just I want to know what will happen at least two days before.

🕮 Dialogue 4

A: Hello, Mr. Kim. How may I help you?

B: I'm calling to confirm an appointment for this evening.

A: OK. Is it at 7:30 this evening at Su-Ra, Korean restaurant, Sir?

B: That's right.

A: I will be expecting you very soon, Sir.

B: Thank you for helping me.

A: You're welcome, Sir.

🕮 Dialogue 5

A: Jim, what are you going to do tonight?

B: Nothing special.

A: Let's have dinner tonight. Are you free tonight?

B: Well, actually, I have to finish my assignment.

A: That's a pity! How about tomorrow instead?

B: Great. Where and what time shall we meet tomorrow?

A: Let's shall meet at 7:00 at the bar near my office.

B: OK, see you there.

04 Telephone

전화

O·V·E·R·V·I·E·W

인간은 커뮤니케이션을 할 때 언어적 수단과 비언어적 수단을 사용한다. 이때 의사소통과 의미의 전달을 위해서 말이나 글을 통한 언어적 수단 외에 표정, 몸짓, 손짓 등의 비언어적 수단이 아주 중요한 역할을 한다. 실제로 영어가 모국어가 아닌 많은 사람들이 전화통화를 할 때 상대방 말을 잘 알아듣지 못하는 이유는 상대방의 목소리 톤이나 어조에만 집중을 하기 때문이다. 따라서 전화상의 대화는 반드시 기본적 표현을 익히고 6하 원칙에 따라 상대방의 말을 정확히 알아듣는 것이 중요하다.

Useful Expressions

Making a phone call

Hello. May I speak to Kate, Please?
Hello. I'd like to talk to Tom.
Could I speak to Jack, please.
Could I talk to Mary?
Is John there?
Hello, this is Laura speaking. May I speak to Mr Smith, please?

How to answer

Yes, speaking.
Hello, this is Tom speaking. Who 's calling, please.
She is not here right now.
May I take a message for you?
Would you like to leave a message?
Would you hold on a moment, please? I will put him on.
Please hold the line Sir. I will transfer your call.
Please, don' t hang up.
He' s on the another phone.
I' m afraid you' ve got the wrong number.
I' m sorry. I can' t hear you.
The line is busy.
I couldn' t get through.
Could you put me on the extension 225, please.
Let me see if he' s in the office.
Someone is asking for you on the phone.

Ending

Thank you for booking with us. I am looking forward to seeing you soon.
I will call back later(again).
Thanks for calling.
Please call me later.

Tip

전화상으로 통화를 하다가 잘 알아듣지 못하면 pardon me?, Excuse me?, Please say again, I' m sorry, would you repeat slowly? 등으로 말할 수 있다. 전화를 걸 때는 Long distance call(장거리 전화), Local call(지역 내 전화), overseas call(국제전화), country code number(국가번호), telephone charge(전화요금), telephone operator(교환원), cellular phone(휴대폰), cordless phone(무선전화기) 등의 표현이 있다.

Dialogue

Dialogue 1

A: Hello.

B: Hello, may I speak to John, please.

A: Who's calling, please?

B: This is Tim, his friend.

A: Just hold on a line, Mr. Tim.

C: This is John speaking.

B: How are you, John?

C: I'm great, thank you. And you?

B: Good. Are you free tonight? If you are, please come over to our place. We are having a barbecue party.

C: That sounds great.

B: What time can I pick you up?

C: Is it OK at 5: 30pm?

B: I'll see you later, Bye.

🕮 Dialogue 2

A: Good evening! Welcome to J&L Hotel. How may I help you?
B: Hello, I want to make a reservation, please.
A: How long are you staying here, sir?
B: For two nights?
A: Certainly Sir. When are you planning to stay with us?
B: It will be from 15th of December to 16th of December.
A: Do you need a single or double?
B: I need a double.
A: I will check for you sir. Just a moment, please.
We have double room available from 15th to 16th.
B: That's good. Would it be possible to have a room with sea-side view?
A: Certainly, we can do it for you.

🕮 Dialogue 3

A: Hello, is this Hyatt hotel? I want to have a non-smoking room for tonight, please.
B: Yes, We have a non-smoking room available tonight. May I have your name, please?
A: My name is Andrew Chang.
B: May I have your phone number please?
A: My mobile number is 555 3452.
B: Is there anything else I can do it for you, sir?
A: No that's all. Thank you.
B: Thank you for booking with us. I'll see you tonight, sir.

Dialogue 4

A: Hello, this is Jennifer speaking. May I speak to Mr. Kim, please?

B: I'm sorry. He's on another line at the moment. May I take a message, Ms. Jennifer?

A: Well, would you ask him to call me back as soon as possible?

B: Sure, can I have your number?

A: He has my number.

B: I will give Mr. Kim your message as soon as he finishes the call.

A: Thanks.

Dialogue 5

A: Hello, Suzy. It's Tom. How are you today?

B: Hi, Tom. I'm not well. I got a cold and I've been staying at home all day long.

A: That's too bad. I've been trying to get hold of you. I couldn't get through.

B: Maybe my battery run out.

A: You should take care of yourself. I'll try again this evening, bye.

B: Thanks for calling, bye.

05 Travel

여행

O·V·E·R·V·I·E·W

여행지를 선정하고 여행 계획을 세우는 일은 아주 신나는 일이다. 여행지에 대한 정보와 함께 예약시 여행일자와 이용하고자 하는 운송 편명을 정확히 체크를 하여 출발하는 것이 중요하다. 출발일자(departure date), 도착일자(arrival date), 출발지(port of boarding), 목적지(destination 혹은 port of landing), 운송 편명(courier number)을 정확하게 미리 알아두어야만 즐거운 여행을 마칠 수 있을 것이다. 해외에서도 여행지의 매너를 잘 지킴으로서 추한 한국인(Ugly Korean)이 되지 않도록 하자.

Useful Expressions

Request

Can you give me a sight-seeing guide book?
Can you tell me something about interesting places for sightseeing?
Would you take a package tour or travel alone?

Offer

I would like to recommend....

This place is the most popular place...

If you consider your budget of travel expenses...

In case you don't have to consider too much on your travel expenses...

What I know about this place....

Tip

여행자들은 단체로 혹은 개별 여행을 하는가에 따라서 group traveller와 FIT(foreign independent traveller)로 나뉜다. Single trip과 round trip은 one-way trip과 two-ways trip으로 편도와 왕복 여행을 말한다. 이때 return ticket은 돌아오는 왕복편 티켓을 말한다.

Dialogue

Planning for your trip

A: I am go to Japan for a week. But I don't know where to go and how to get there.
B: Do you want to take a package tour or travel alone?
A: I thought about taking a package tour.
B: I Can recommend the Korea Tour to you? Just tell them when you want to go, and they will take care about your trip.
A: Thanks. Can I have the phone number?
B: It's 4430-8891

Making a reservation

A: Hello, is this Korea Tour agent? I need to book a tour to Japan.
B: Where do you want to go and how long would you like your trip?
A: I want to go on a tour of Tokyo during the first week of May.
B: We can book you for a flight to Tokyo on May first. You'll stay for 4 days in Tokyo to visit all the famous tourist attractions.
A: How much is the tour?
B: 800 dollars for each person.
A: What does it include?
B: It includes your air fare, hotel accommodations and three meals each day.
A: That sounds interesting. Could you do that for me?

About business trips

A: Good morning!
B: Good morning! What can I do for you?
A: I plan to go to the annual tourism exposition in New York in April.
B: Sure. We can handle your matters including hotel reservations and transportation in New York.
Is someone to accompany you on your visit to New York?
A: No one, I'm going to Texas to have a meeting with local tourist board afterwards.
B: You'll fly on KoreanAir from Seoul to New York. The flight will take about 11 hours and you'll arrive in there for dinner. And your next flight to Texas will be scheduled on your time table.
A: Thank you for helping me.
B: Anytime.

Booking a flight

A: Good morning. Can I help you?
B: I need to make a reservation to Paris for March 2.
A: Just a moment, please, Sir. Let me check the flight schedule for you.
B: Alright.
A: I'm so sorry, sir. There is no ticket available on that day. But we do have a flight for Paris next day.
B: I have no choice. Would you book me on the flight?
A: Sure. Would you like a single trip or round trip?
B: I prefer a round trip.
A: Right, sir. And please don't forget to bring a valid passport when you go on the flight.
B: I will.

06 Airport

공항

O·V·E·R·V·I·E·W

비행기를 이용하여 다른 나라로 여행을 간다는 것은 정말 기분 좋은 일이다. 요즘은 장거리 노선(long-haul flight)과 단거리 노선(short-haul flight)을 비행기로 이용하는데 가격이 저렴한 저가항공사(low fare airlines 혹은 budget airlines)와 할인제도(frequent flyers program)를 이용하고 있다. 직항노선(direct flight)과 연결노선(transit flight)을 이용하여 빠른 시간으로 저렴하게 세계 곳곳을 여행하는 것은 매력적인 일이다. 공항에서의 업무는 이러한 승객들의 취항준비(airline fight), 체크인(check in), 보안(security), 출입국(immigration), 세관(customs), 검역(quarantine) 등을 담당을 하고 있다.

Useful Expressions

Check-in

Where should I check-in?
Where is check-in counter?
May I have your passport and ticket, please?
How many pieces of baggage do you have?
How many pieces of baggage do you want to check in?
Do you have any luggage to check in?
Could you place your luggage in here, please?
No carts beyond this line.
When is the boarding time?
Here are your ticket and boarding pass.
What time will we start boarding?
We will begin boarding at 2:20 at Gate 15.

Security

Please put all your belongings in this basket, please?
Step aside, please.
Could you raise your arms please?
Would you mind opening your brief case?

Boarding

This is the boarding announcement for flight 777 bound for Sydney.
All passenger using flight 777 to Sydney, please proceed to gate 54.
This is the line for business class.
Would you show me your boarding pass, please?
Priority for disable person and children.

Destination

What is the purpose of your visit?
I am here on business.
I am on transit to Mexico.
It will be automatically transferred to your next flight.
Where is the baggage claim area?
Where can I pick up my bag?
It will be coming on the next flight.
Please, fill out the customs declaration (form).
Do you have anything to declare?
Do you have something to declare, cigarette or liquorer?
I have nothing to declare.

Tip

한국으로 입국 시에 입국신고서와 세관신고서를 반드시 작성하여야 한다. 외국인은 한 장의 입국신고서를 작성하고, 세관신고서는 내/외국인 모두 한 가족 당 한 장씩 작성하면 된다. 입국 시 신고해야할 품목으로 해외 총 취득가격이 U$400불(미화) 이상의 초과 물품이다. 1인당 면세 기준은 주류 1병, 담배 10갑, 향수 2온스에 한해 면세된다. 다음에 제시되는 단어들은 반드시 알고 있어야 할 것이다.
Passport, Immigration form, Customs declaration form, Nothing to declare, Something to declare, Quarantine

Dialogue

📖 Dialogue 1

A: May I see your passport and ticket, please?
B: Here you are.
A: Would you prefer aisle or window seat?
B: I want to have a aisle seat, please.
A: How many pieces of baggage do you have?
B: I have two.
A: Could you place your language in here, please?
B: Yes.
A: Here is your boarding pass. Your departure gate will be gate 55. And your departure time is 7:50.
B: Thank you.

🕮 Dialogue 2

A: Good morning. How can I help you?

B: I'd like to check the flight time to Paris.

A: I'm sorry, sir. The flight has been delayed for 30 mins.

B: Really. What happen?

A: Because of the bad weather condition in New York international airport. You have to wait at the boarding gate. I'm sorry for causing any trouble, sir.

B: I don't have a choice right now. I'll wait until the boarding announcement comes on.

A: I'm so sorry for causing inconvenience.

🕮 Dialogue 3

A: I need to cancel my flight to Paris for May 5. I need to reschedule my flight.

B: Give me a minute, please. I'll check for you, sir.

A: Is there a penalty for changing my plans?

B: There will be no penalty for it. But when do you want to fly to Paris?

A: May 6.

B: I'm sorry, there is no ticket available on that day. But we have flights for Paris the next day.

A: Would you book me on the morning flight?

B: How about a 9:15 flight?

A: That will be fine.

🕮 Dialogue 4

A: How long are you staying in America?
B: I have six days.
A: Is this your first time visit to America?
B: No, I'd visited several times.
A: What do you do for a living?
B: I'm a scientist.
A: Where do you stay in?
B: I'm staying at Plaza hotel in New York.
A: What's your purpose of visit to America.
B: I'm on business. I am going to attend Science Fair for the time.
A: OK. You have a nice trip in America. Thanks.

🕮 Dialogue 5

A: Do you have anything to declare?
B: Yes, I have something to declare. I have a bottle of Korean liquor. It's for my friend in America.
A: What's the approximate value?
B: About 20dollars.
A: Anything else, sir?
B: That's about it.
A: You have a pleasant day!

🕮 Dialogue 6

A: Do we have to fill in this form?

B: It's I-94 form to fill in.

A: What should I do after filling in the form?

B: You should hand it to immigration officer in airport after landing.

A: What happen after we go through immigration?

B: You have to go the baggage claim area, then pass the customs.

A: Thanks for your information.

B: You're welcome.

07 In the airplane

비행기 안

O·V·E·R·V·I·E·W

객실 서비스는 크게 3가지로 승객을 환영하고(greeting), 서비스를 제공하고(serving), 돌보는 것(attending passenger)으로 구성되어 있다. 이러한 3가지 외에도 승객들을 편안(comforting)하게 하고, 기내 방송(cabin announcement), 면세품 판매(duty-free sales), 각종 기내식과 음료의 제공(food and beverage service) 및 다양한 개인적 서비스(a personal service to passenger)를 수행한다.

Useful Expressions

Excuse me, but I am afraid this is my seat.
Would you mind changing your seat with me?
Do you mind if I put my seat back?
Put your seats to the upright position.
Please fasten your seat belts.
May I get through?
Do you have anything to read?
Excuse me, I don't have a headset.

Could you put my bag in the overhead compartment?
This headphone is out of order.
Would you like something to drink?
May I have a coke, please?
Which would you like beef or chicken?
What would you like to have?
I am vegetarian.
I' m sorry, but we are out of beef.
Each person has to fill out the landing card.
Excuse me, what should I write here?
I made some mistakes, may I have another immigration form?

Tip

기내에서는 다양한 기내식과 음료가 제공된다. 기내식은 종교상, 건강상 등의 이유로 특별식을 요청할 수 있는데, 반드시 비행기가 출발하기 전 항공권을 예약할 때 미리 주문하여야한다. 또한 어린이들을 위한 Children' s menu, 채식주의자들을 위한 Vegetarian meal, 유대인들을 위한 Kosher meal, 당뇨를 가진 분들을 위한 Diabetic meal 외에도 특별식으로 No-cholesterol meal, Strick vegetarian meal, High protein meal, Baby food 등이 제공된다. 또한 기내에서 다양한 음악과 영화채널, 게임을 즐길 수 있으며, 간식으로 한국라면, 아이스크림, 캔디와 초콜릿, 쿠키 등도 즐길 수 있다.

Dialogue

🕮 Boarding

S: Welcome on board. Sir. May I have your boarding pass, please?
P: Here it is. Where is my seat?
S: Your seat is 40B, aisle seat. Come this way, please. I'll show you to the seat.
P: Thanks a lot.
S: Please, put your bag in the over-head compartment. I'll help you with it.
P: All right.
S: If you need anything else during the flight, please let us know.
(P: Passenger S: Stewardess)

🕮 Take- off

S: Excuse me, sir. We're going to take off in a moment. Would you please return your seat to the upright position?
Thank you for your cooperation.
P: What's the actual flight time from Seoul to Los Angeles?
S: It depends on the weather condition, but it usually takes about ten hours.
P: I see.
S: Please keep your seat belts fasten until the captain has turned off the seat belt sign.
P: Of course.

In-flight service

S: Which would you like to have for dinner, beef or pork?

P: I'll have beef. By the way could you bring me a menu?

S: It's in the seat pocket in front of you. Would you care for something to drink, sir?

P: Beer, please.

S: What kind of beer do you want?

P: Do you have Hite?

S: Certainly, here is your beer.
Anything else, Sir? Enjoy your meal.

In-flight movie

P: What's the arrival time?

S: We'll be arriving at 8pm in Paris at local time.

P: I see.
What kind of movie are you showing today?

S: It's a comedy. You can find our program in your in-flight magazine.

P: When are you going to show it?

S: We will show the movie after the meal service.

P: If it is possible, can I change the seat?

S: Of course, Sir. I'll look for an available seat for you, sir.

Handling problems

S: I see you call light is on. What can I help you?
P: Yes, I'm not feeling well.
S: What's your problem?
P: I have a bad headache. Do you have aspirin?
S: Certainly. Is there anything else I can do it for you?
P: Not much.
S: I will bring a blanket and warm water for you just in case.
P: Thank you so much.

Attending passengers

P: I think I'll take a short nap before dinner.
S: Let me get you a pillow and blanket from your overhead compartment. Sir, we are taking orders for dinner. Would you prefer chicken or beef?
P: I'd like a beef, please. But my friend is sleeping at the moment. Could you come back later?
S: Sure.

Before landing

S: Excuse me. We'll be landing shortly, please fasten your seat belt. Would you mind keeping your bag under your seat, please.
P: Oh, I see.
S: Did you enjoy the flight today?
P: It was great. Thank you.
S: My pleasure. I hope to see you on board again.

08 Hotel

호텔

O·V·E·R·V·I·E·W

호텔에서 고객들을 직접 응대하는 객실부분(room department)은 프런트서비스(front service), 유니폼서비스(uniformed service), 하우스키핑(housekeeping)으로 나눈다. 프런트 오피스는 예약(reservation), 체크인(check-in)/체크아웃(check-out), 커뮤니케이션(communications), 캐셔서비스(cashier), 컨시야지(concierge) 등으로 구분된다. 유니폼서비스는 도어맨(door man), 벨맨(bell man), 포터(porter), 벨캡틴(bell captain) 등이 호텔의 현관서비스를 담당하고 있다. 하우스키핑은 객실청소(housekeeper and roommaid service), 세탁업무(laundry service), 미니바와 비품관리(checking mini-bar), 객실 및 호텔점검 및 유지(cleaning corridors and public areas)와 관련된 일을 한다.

Useful Expressions

Check-in

Would you please fill in this registration card?
Would you please sign here, sir?
Would you please write your signature here, sir?
What are the rates for the rooms?

Who are you staying with?
What kind of room would you like?
How much is a double room?
How long are you planning to stay here?
How will you be paying, sir?
How many people will be staying, sir?
Is there a room available for tonight?
We have a full house during the peak season.
We are fully booked tonight.
We are booked up for tonight.
Your room is confirmed from July 25th to the 27th.
A single room with fine view, please.
If there isn't any room, we can put you on a waiting list.

Doorman/Bellman service

Could you take care of my bags?
Can you park my car in the parking lot?
I'll get your baggage right away.
No tipping is our policy.
You'll be charged for what you use from mini-bar.
If you require other service, just contact number 5 bell desk.

Communications

I think it is best taking a bus.
How long does it take to get there?
Can you suggest some nice place for our dinner?
The restaurants open at 11am and close at 6pm.
The prices are also reasonable.
Can you make an arrangement for the bus tour of Seoul.

Operator

Can I get a 6:30 wake-up call tomorrow morning?
May I have extension 506, please?
The line is busy at this moment. There is no answer from room 506.
Please keep on trying.
You are connected.
Hold on a moment. I'll transfer your call to Mr. Brown.
I am afraid you have the wrong number.
Please give me your number, I'll call you back.

Check-out

I am ready to check out now.
How much is the charge?
I would like to settle my account.
The guest will pay by credit card.
Would you sign here on the bottom.
This is your change and receipt.
There is something wrong with my bill. It seems very high to me.
Do you want me to check it for you?
Can you make out two separate bills?
One for the room charge and another one for meals.

Housekeeping

I need my room made up.
I will make up you room immediately.
It will take about 25 minutes to clean the room
Would you fix the toilet? It is not working.
I'll send somebody up to your room.
Shall I have some more ice water?
Do you have an iron and board? I need to have my suit pressed.
We don't provide the iron or board but we do have laundry service for that. There is extra charge for that.

Tip

Connecting room과 Adjoining room의 차이는 connecting room은 바로 옆방으로 두 개의 방 사이에 객실 문(connecting door)이 서로 연결되어 있는 경우로 가족 단위로 투숙을 할 때 옆방에 미성년자인 아이들을 잘 보살필 수 있으며, adjoining room은 인접한 방을 말한다. 같은 층에 두 객실이 인접해 있는 것이다.

가족끼리 투숙하거나 정원 이외의 인원이 투숙할 경우 extra bed(여분의 침대)를 요청할 수 있다. 이때는 호텔마다 다르지만 무료 혹은 소정의 요금(미국의 경우 US60~100달러)을 지불하면 된다. 한국의 호텔은 대부분 Single occupancy 즉, 객실 당 요금지불을 원칙으로 한다(pay per room).

Dialogue

Checking-in with reservation

A: Good afternoon, sir! Welcome to Hill Top hotel.

B: Good afternoon! I'd like to have a single room, please.

A: Have you made a reservation?

B: Yes, I have already booked it under the name of Mr. Mike.

A: Please, wait a moment, Mr. Mike. I'll check it for you.
Mr. Mike, a single room for the 27th and the 28th of May.
Would you fill in this registration card.

🕮 Checking-in without reservation

A: Hello, do you have a double room for tonight?

B: One moment please. I'll check for you. I'm afraid we haven't got a double room, sir. We've got five singles and two twins.

A: Well, I'll take the twin room.

B: Sure, May I have your name, please?

A: Harry Kim.

B: How long will you stay for here, sir?

A: I am going to stay for two nights. What are the rates for the room?

B: The rates are right here on the tariff card, sir.

A: I see.

B: Would you fill in the registration form.

A: Here you are.

B: I hope you enjoy staying here with us.

🕮 Doorman service

A: Good morning? May I help you with your baggage?

B: Yes, Here are my baggage. please.

A: Certainly, madam. Just leave them here and I'll take care of yours. Please, come this way to the front desk.

B: Thank you.

A: It's my pleasure. Enjoy your stay. sir.

Doorman service

A: Good morning, Sir. Welcome to Mariett hotel.
May I help you with your luggage?
B: No, thanks. It's not so heavy. I can manage it.
Where can I register?
A: The front desk is over there to your right. You won't miss it.
B: Thanks.
A: You are welcome, sir.

Bellman service

A: I'll show you to your room.
B: Thanks.
A: Here, we are on the 7th floor. Your room is 705.
B: It's a very nice room.
A: I'm glad you like it.
The bathroom is here and the closet is over there, Sir.
B: I would like to get some mineral water and beer.
A: You can get it from mini-bar in the room, Sir. The mini bar is fully stocked with liquor, beer and soft drinks.
B: Oh, I see.
A: Is there anything else I can do for you, Sir?
B: That's all.
A: If you need any help, please feel free to call us.
B: I'll do that. Thanks for your help.

🕮 Bellman service

A: How can I get to Korean restaurant?

B: We have Sura Korean restaurant on the basement. The prices are also reasonable.

A: Really? How late does the restaurant stay open?

B: We do open until midnight.

A: Do we need to reserve a table?

B: You better do. Can I book a table for you? What time would you like to go there, Sir?

A: 7 pm.

B: I'll do that for you.

🕮 Communications

A: Good morning, what can I help you?

B: My name is Ted Baker in room 506.
Is there any message for me?

A: Please, wait a moment, Sir.
Yes, there is a message for you.
Mr. Mike wants you to call him.

B: I was supposed to meet him here at 4pm. How long did he wait?

A: For about 30 minutes.

B: Oh, no! I was completely lost. I should call him right now and apologize to him.

Communications

A: Hello, this is Hyatt hotel how may I help you?
B: What time do you serve lunch at restaurants?
A: From 12 o'clock, Sir. From 12 till 2:30 in both restaurants.
B: Where are the places?
A: One is on the ground floor, and the other is on the second floor.
B: Is room service available too?
A: Sure, the room service is 24-hour service. You can ring form your room, Sir.
B: Thank you for your information.

Concierge

A: Can I get some tour information?
B: Yes, Sir. What can I help you?
A: I'd like to take a city tour in Seoul. Would you recommend me some nice places?
B: We have a shuttle bus leaving in front of hotel. It covers several tourist attractions around Seoul. The bus leaves at 10am and runs every 2 hours.
A: That's good. Do I have to buy a ticket?
B: No, you don't need. It's free of charge for our guests.
Would you just confirm your party.
A: Three of us.
B: OK. I'll see you tomorrow morning, sir.

🕮 Concierge

A: Would you tell me the best to way to go to airport?
B: Yes, I think you'd better take a subway.
A: Where is the nearest subway station?
B: Just in front of hotel.
A: How long does it take to go there by subway?
B: It usually takes about 40 minutes.
A: I see. I should take a subway rather than taking a taxi.

🕮 Operator

A: Good afternoon, this is your operator. Can I help you?
B: I'd like to speak to Mr. Jones, please. This is Brown, one of his colleagues.
A: Wait a second. I'll put you through to the front desk.
C: Hello, front desk. May I help you?
B: Yes, I want to talk to Mr. Jones.
C: Would you spell the last name, Sir?
B: J-O-N-E-S.
C: Thank you very much.
Please don't hang up and I'll connect you right away.
Mr. Jones is on the line.
B: Thank you.

🕮 Operator

A: Good evening, Hyatt hotel. How may I help you?

B: Yes, this is Mike Hong in room 829. Could you give me a wake-up call at 7:00 tomorrow morning, please.

A: Of course, Mr. Hong. We'll give you a wake-up call at that time.

B: Thanks a lots.

🕮 Checking-out

A: Good morning, how was your stay, Sir?

B: It was great. I want to check out now.

A: Just a moment, Sir. Here is your bill. Did you get something from your mini bar?

B: I have a bottle of mineral water and a beer.

A: Your total bill comes to 310 dollars altogether, Sir.

B: It seems very high to me. Would you give me the details?

A: Certainly. 150 dollars from your room charge, 10 dollars from mini bar, 150 dollars from restaurant bill including taxes and service charges.

B: I see, I'd like to pay by credit card.

A: Very well, can I have you card, please.

B: Here you are.

A: It's all settled. I hope you had a pleasant stay here. I am looking forward to seeing you again, Sir.

Checking-out

A: I'm checking out today. Will you make out my bill?
B: Certainly.
A: I also want to change US dollars into Korean won. What's the rate today?
B: The exchange rate is 1180 won for one dollar. How much do you want to change?
A: Two hundred dollars. Do you think is it enough for meals in Korea?
B: It depends where you want to eat. Would you fill out this form and show me your passport, please.
A: I see.
B: Would you tell me write your room number and name, Sir.

Housekeeping

A: This is Tom Jones, room 827. Could you send someone up? My television doesn't work.
B: Is it plugged in?
A: Yes, I checked it. How long do I have to wait?
B: Right away, Sir.
A: That's good. Thanks.

🕮 Housekeeping

A: Housekeeping, May I help you?

B: Yes, I need my room cleaned up now.

A: What's your room number, Sir?

B: 305.

A: I'll send a room-maid up to your room immediately.
Do you want anything else, Sir?

B: At the same time, can you send a extra blanket?

A: Sure and there are also extra pillows and blankets in the closet.

B: I appreciate it.

A: Don't mention it, Sir.

🕮 Lost and found service

A: Can I help you?

B: I think I've lost my pen.

A: Do you know where you lost it?

B: I'm not very sure. I used it when I checked bill in restaurant downstairs.

A: I'll check there and also check the lost and found.

B: Please, do it for me.

A: I'm sorry for what happened. I'll make sure to contact you if it's found.

🕮 Laundry service

A: Laundry service, can I help you?

B: Yes, I need my shirts and pants to be cleaned and pressed.

A: I'll send someone over to your room.

B: I'm about to go out now.

A: You can just put it into a laundry bag and hang outside of your door.

B: Do I have to fill out a laundry form?

A: Yes, Sir. When do you want it to be delivered?

B: I'd like to get it back tomorrow morning. I have to go to a meeting early.

A: We have an express service to be delivered by midnight. But they'll be an extra charge for the service.

B: No problems.

09 Restaurant

식당

O·V·E·R·V·I·E·W

서양요리는 다양한 소스와 드레싱을 사용하고 고기의 구운 정도에 따라 개인 식성에 맞게 주문할 수 있다. 패스트푸드(fast-food) 음식에서부터 프렌치 레스토랑(french Restaurant), 카페테리아(cafeteria), 비스트로(bistro), 커피하우스(Coffee-house), 피자레스토랑(pizza restaurant), 오리엔탈레스토랑(oriental restaurant), 케밥하우스(kebab house) 등 다양한 장소에서 적절한 어구를 구사함으로 즐거운 식사를 마칠 수 있다.

Useful Expressions

Before entering a restaurant

How large is your party?
How many are there in your party?
What time do you open for lunch?
Do you have a reservation, Sir/Madam?
I'd like to book a table for four at 12 o' clock.
Can I have a table by window?
I' ve made a reservation.
Table for two, please.
We open at 12 noon and close at 4 p.m, Sir.

📖 Eat and drink

Can I have a menu please?
Do you have a wine list?
What kind of seafood do you have?
What would you recommend for us?
What is special today?
What's really good?
Would you like something to drink?

📖 Taking an order

Are you ready to order?
What would you like to have?
How would you like your steak?
Would you like to have any dessert?
Can I offer you something to drink?
How do you like your egg?
This is your wine, Sir/Madam.
I will try this one, please.
I want to have my steak well-done, please.(rare, medium, well-done)
Over easy, please.(scrambled, sunny-side up, boiled, poached, fried)
I'd like a glass of wine.
I prefer a scotch on the rocks or a dry wine.
Give me another.
I'll have a beer.

Finishing a meal

Is there anything I can get for you?
Do you need anything else?
Can I have my bill, please?
Do you accept credit card here?
I will bring it here for you.
It was a great meal!
I've eaten too much.
I'm really full.

Tip

외국에서는 탄산음료를 주문할 때 코크(coke), 세븐업(seven-up), 스프라이트(sprite)로 부른다. 이러한 음료는 비알코올성 음료로써 소프트 드링크(soft-drinks)라고 하며, 젊은 사람들 사이에서 'pop'이라고 불린다. pop은 '갑자기 펑 터진다', 마개를 뽑으면 '발포한다'는 의미에서 사용되었으며, 샴페인, 스파클링 와인, 탄산을 포함한 청량음료를 지칭한다.

Dialogue

Dialogue 1

A: Good evening! How may I help you?

B: Hello, I need a table for two, please.

A: Do you have a reservation Sir?

B: Yes, I did it, yesterday. Under the name of Lee.

A: Yes, certainly, we have your reservation.

B: Thank you

A: I will show you to your table.

B: Could you give us a nice window table?

A: Certainly, we can do it for you. Come this way, Sir.

B: Thank you.

A: Here you are. Would you like something to drink before you order anything?

B: I will have diet coke, please.

A: I will leave you for a moment, when you are ready to order just call us, please.

B. Yes, I will.

Dialogue 2

A: Would you care for drinks while you wait?

B: Do you have non-alcoholic drinks?

A: Of course, we have a choice of juices, soft drinks and coffee or tea.

B: A diet coke please. Make that two.

🕮 Dialogue 3

A: Would you like to order now, Sir?
B: Just give me a minute. Well, what's special today?
A: We have a clam chowder soup, and we also have fish with asparagus and boiled potatoes.
B: Is the fish spicy?
A: A little bit.
B: Sounds great. I'll have the fish.
A: Is there anything else to drink?
B: A glass of house wine please.
A: I'll come back in a few minutes.

🕮 Dialogue 4

A: What's on the menu today?
B: We have stake, chicken, fish, vegetables and potatoes.
A: I want to have stake and potatoes, please.
B: How would you like your steak, Sir?
A: I will have medium to well-done please.
B: What about potatoes, Sir? Baked, boiled, mashed, and fried?
A: Baked will be fine.
B: What kind of dressing on your salad?
A: What do you have?
B: We have italian, thousand island, greek, french ranch, oil and vinegar, and house.
A: I'll try oil and vinegar, please.
B: Sure, your dinner will be ready in five minutes.

Dialogue 5

A: Have you finished your meal? How was your meal?
B: It was great!! Especially, the mutton chop was very good.
A: Happy to hear that. Would you like to have some dessert?
We have pecan pie.
B: That's good idea. Could you serve a cup of coffee, please.
A: How would you like your coffee?
B: Coffee with milk.
After that, can I have my bill please.

Dialogue 6

A: I'd like two chicken burgers and one coke with plenty of ice, please.
B: Eat-in or to go?
A: To go, please.
B: Anything else? What about some dessert?
A: No thanks, that's enough for me.

Dialogue 7

A: Have you anything in mind to order your drinks, Sir?
B: I don't want alcoholic drinks. Well, I'm not sure there's some soft drinks.
A: What kind of soft drink would you like to have?
B: I'll have a fresh mango juice. Do you have that?
A: Certainly. How about you, miss?
C: I'll order a beer as usual.
A: Here are your beer and juice. Enjoy your drinks!

Dialogue 8

A: Would you care to order for breakfast?
B: I'll have a morning buffet.
A: All right. Would like to have something to drink?
B: Coffee please.
A: How would like your coffee?
B: Make it black. (Or, coffee with sugar but no cream)
A: Would like anything else, madam? Would like some more coffee?
C: Yes, a little more coffee will be great.
A: How was your breakfast?
B: That was lovely.
A: I'm glad you enjoyed it.
B: May I have the check, please.
A: Certainly, I'll be back right away.

10 Cooking

요리

O·V·E·R·V·I·E·W

한국음식을 외국인들에게 소개한다는 것은 너무나 자랑스러운 일이다. 한국 음식은 오랜 전통과 역사를 가지고 있으며, 뛰어난 맛과 균형적인 영양성분을 함유하고 있는 우수한 음식이다. 특히 미국에서는 한국음식을 건강식이며 영양식이고 높은 품격을 가진 문화음식이라고 높이 평가했다.

Useful Expressions

About cuisines

Korean cuisine is famous for spicy food.
Sichuan cuisine is noted for its hot flavors.
Japanese food is famous for raw fish and their original flavors.
Korean cooking style is known for its wide variety of ingredients and unique flavor.
Italian cooking is very popular in the United States.
We are focusing on food' s nutrition, colors and textures.

In the kitchen

How many covers do we have this morning?
Could you start with salad section, please?
I will take those to the buffet section.
It will be a lot of work today.
Could you finish this stock for me?
I will have to start this.
Be careful with this.
Could you be able to check dessert section.
Is there anything we need to fill it up?
Could you make more of egg fried? It will be six portions.
Could you service this dish? Services (dishes) are ready!
Could you be able to check with this order? I am not sure with this.

Cooking skills

Braise the potatoes.
Saute the onions.
I like stir-fried beef in Sichuan style.
First brown the meat and then add vegetables.
Garlic and chilli are essential for Korean Kimchi.
We need some minced beef and chopped tomatoes to make spaghetti.
Is the sauce ready?
Wait until the oil is hot.

Tip

한국음식을 먹을 때도 서양의 식사매너처럼 지켜야 할 예절이 있다. 외국인과 식사 시 이러한 우리의 식사문화를 정확히 알려주면 식사가 보다 즐거울 것이다. 밥그릇은 손으로 들고 먹지 않으며, 음식을 먹을 때 수저 소리를 내지 않는다. 식사 중 코를 풀지 않으며(서양에서는 허용됨), 기침과 재채기 시에 옆으로 얼굴을 돌려 손이나 손수건으로 가린다. 연장자가 먼저 수저를 든 후에 시작하며, 상대방과 속도를 맞추어 식사를 거의 동시에 마칠 수 있도록 하자.

Dialogue

Dialogue 1

A: Good morning, today we are expecting 600 covers. We need to move faster. David, Could you start with scramble egg. Kate, please check cold buffet section and if they are ready, could you start to bring cold food out there?

B & C: I'll do it right away

A: Where did you put service dishes?

C: They are over there chef.

A: David, could you start with main dish. Please also check with them, they call main dish away for table 14.

B: Yes, chef.

A: Ok, there will be no more special dishes left for tonight.

C: I will tell them, right away.

Dialogue 2

A: What are you cooking?
B: Fish
A: Can I help you?
B: Not really.
A; Do you like cooking?
B: It's fun to cook.
A: Do you prepare for your dessert?
B: I haven't decided yet what to make.
A: How about apple pie. I'm good at making pie.
B: Would you teach me how to make apple pie?
A: Yes. Take some milk, some flour, add some sugar. Cut some apples and then mix everything together.
(.........)
A: Smells so good. Let's try some fish and apple pie.

Dialogue 3

A: Smells great! What's cooking?
B: I'm making a cheese pizza with homemade french fries and garlic bread.
A: Do you really know how to use oven?
B: Yes, preheat the oven first, then leave it up for 20 mins.
A: Great. did you freshly cut some potatoes into strips?
B: Yes. It's very easy to make a delicious food at home.

🕮 Dialogue 4

A: Would you recommend me a Korean food?
B: Do you like beef?
A: Of course.
B: Beef ribs is very popular in Korea, which is marinated in a sauce and grilled for a really special meal.
A: What are the ingredients?
B: There are say sauce, sliced ginger, grounded onion and pear, chopped garlic, some sesame oil and pepper, and of course beef ribs.
A: Wow, it sounds delicious.
B: You will love it.

🕮 Dialogue 5

A: Can you tell me how to make a nice red-tea?
B: Yes, with my pleasure. First get the boiling water ready. Before you put some dried leaves in a pot, warm the pot with hot water and drain it out. Put some tea leaves into the pot and leave them for four minutes.
A: Could I add some milk or a slice of lemon into it?
B: It's up to you. Some people like black tea. I, however, prefer to have tea with milk.
A: How often do you drink tea?
B: I drink several cups of tea a day and I do really like the aroma.

Dialogue 6

A: Have you decided what to order?

B: What is popular in Korea?

A: It depends what you like. Would you prefer beef or chicken dish?

B: Do you have anything else besides beef or chicken?

A: Well, how about vegetable dish? We have Japchae and Bibimbap.

B: Could you kindly explain what it's about?

A: Sure. Japchae is potato noodles stir-fried with vegetables such spinach, mushroom, egg strips, carrot and onion. The recipe is just as delicious with the larger variety.

B: Can it be vegetarian meal?

A: Of course, you can order the dish without sliced beef.

B: Is Bibimbap also vegetarian meal?

A: A kind of. Bibimbap is a rice dish served with vegetables and sometimes meat to mix in the bowl at the table. You can add chilli sauce and sesame oil if you like a spicy food.

Part Ⅱ

Grammar

01 8품사(Parts of Speech), 문장의 구성요소

정말 중요합니다. 완전히 익혀질 때까지 익히고 익혀야 할 것입니다.

우리가 다른 사람과의 의사소통을 위해서는 머릿속으로 문장을 만들어 의미전달을 해야 하고 여기서 우리가 만들어내는 문장은 여러 가지의 요소로 구성되어 있다. 이러한 구성요소들은 각기 다른 기능을 가지고 있고 그 기능별 분류를 8품사라고 한다.

8품사에는 대명사, 명사, 동사, 형용사, 부사, 감탄사, 접속사. 전치사가 있다. 나중에 설명하겠지만 문장을 구성하는 필수요소가 될 수 있는 8품사는 앞의 네 가지인 대명사, 명사, 동사, 형용사들이고 나머지 부사, 감탄사, 접속사, 전치사는 문장성문에 포함되지 않는다.

대명사(Pronoun)	명사(Noun)	동사(Verb)	형용사(Adjective)
명사 대신 사용되는 말. 문장에서 주어와 목적어가 될 수 있다.	세상 모든 것들의 이름. 문장에시 주이와 목적어가 될 수 있다.	사물의 동작이나 상태를 나타냄. 문장에서 동시의 역할을 함.	명사나 대명사를 수식, 서술. 문장에서 보어 역할을 함.
Ex) 인칭 He, She 관계 who 재귀 himself 지시 it this 부정 one, another	Ex) 보통, 집합, 고유, 물질, 추상	Ex) 현재형, 과거형 미래형(규칙변화 : -ed), 불규칙 변화	Ex) pretty, cute

부사(Adverb)	감탄사(Interjection)	접속사(Conjunction)	전치사(Preposition)
동사, 형용사, 부사, 문장의 앞뒤에서 수식하는 말.	감정을 나타내는 말.	양쪽을 접속해주는 역할을 하는 말.	명사, 대명사 앞에 위치하고 장소, 방향, 시간, 방법, 이유 등을 나타냄.
Ex) always, fast, slowly, usually, There, Here	Ex) Yeah, Oh, wow	Ex) And, Or, But, Either, A or B Not only, but also	Ex) at, in, for, from, under

사전을 이용하여 각 단어의 뜻을 찾고 큰소리로 단어를 5번씩 읽어 보자.

위에서 익힌 8품사는 이후 문장의 구성요소라는 문장의 기본요소의 역할을 하게 된다. 여기서 문장의 구성요소라는 것이 무엇인지 알아야 할 것이다. 8품사가 문장의 가장 기본요소라면 구성요소는 이러한 요소를 이용하여 문장을 실제적으로 구성하는 것들을 말한다. 다음의 그림을 보자.

8품사 → 문장의 구성요소 → 문장 → 의미전달

문장을 구성하는 기본적인 요소(문장의 구성요소)에는 주어, 술어, 목적어(간접목적어, 직접목적어), 보어(주격 보어, 목적격 보어)가 있다. 즉 이러한 요소들의 결합을 통해 우리가 다른 사람에게 의사를 전달할 수 있게 된다. 구성요소는 반드시 그 원칙을 지켜서 문장을 만들어야 하는데 여기서 만들어지는 원칙을 문장의 5형식이라고 한다. 문장의 5형식은 다음 장에서 설명할 것이다.

과제

8품사 별로 각자 사전을 통해 단어 20가지씩 찾아 오기

단어장 만들기

실전 문제

※ 밑줄 친 단어의 품사를 말하시오.

1. Liz and Marry went to the U.K

2. I like my friends

3. She is very smart

4. I love her

5. My dog is cute

6. Wow I love this!!

7. You can have this or that

8. I ate lunch at noon

글쓰기를 위한 팁

단어장이 꼭 필요한가에 대한 많은 이야기들이 있다. 실제로 영국의 옥스퍼드와 캠브리지 대학교에 입학하는 유학생들(영어가 모국어가 아닌 사람)의 대부분이 영어공부를 위해 단어장을 활용했다고 한다. 필자의 경험으로 미루어 봐서도 이러한 단어장의 필요성은 너무나 자명해진다.
그럼 단어장이 필요한 건 사실인 것 같은데,, 서점에서 파는 단어장을 활용하면 어떨까 하는 의문에 대해서는 그 활용도나 학습하는 사람들의 기억에 얼마나 오래 갈 것인가에 대해 조금은 의문이 든다. 물론 잘 정돈되고 컴퓨터로 작업까지 마쳤다고 하니 당연히 출제율도 높겠지만 거기에 나오는 문장까지 전부 암기하지 않는 이상은 그 실효성에 대해 더 많은 의구심을 가지게 된다. 쉽게 생각해서 우리가 조그마한 아이에게 사과라는 한 단어를 가르치기 위해 얼마나 많은 시간과 반복을 거듭하는지를 생각해보라. 단어를 자신의 것으로 소화하기 위해서는 그리고 그 단어의 활용을 통해 훌륭한 작문을 하기 위해서는 개인만의 단어장을 만들고 한번이라도 더 써보고 읽어 보아야 한다. 자신이 읽은 문장에서 몰랐던 단어를 알려고 고민한 단어가 더 오래 기억에 남고 활용가능성이 있을 것이라는 것은 너무나 당연한 사실처럼 다가온다.
자! 오늘부터 단어장을 만듭시다. 그리고 단어장에 단어하고 한글 뜻만 쓰지 말고, 발음기호, 예문 그리고 오늘 배운 품사 적는 것 잊지 맙시다.

단어장 적는 법 실례

boy [boi] 명사

뜻: ① 소년, [동의어] lad, youth.

(구어) 남자, 녀석(fellow).

예문: a ~s' school 남자 학교.

02 문장의 형식(Sentence Pattern)

우리가 의사전달을 위해 꼭 해야 하는 말들을 묶어 놓은 것을 문장이라고 한다. 이 문장은 일정한 형식을 가지게 되는데 영어에서는 5가지 문장의 형식이 있고 이것을 문장의 5형식이라고 한다. 영어의 모든 문장은 5형식을 벗어나지 않는다.

문장은 필수성분인 주어, 동사, 목적어, 보어와 부가적인 성분인 수식어로 이루어져 있다.

여기서 문장의 성분을 하나하나 살펴보면

문장성분	종류 및 역할/품사 중 문장성분이 될 수 있는 것	예제
주어 Subject	문장의 주체를 의미, 모든 문장에 필요함 명사, 대명사	Birds sing
동사 Verb	문장의 주체가 하는 행동이나 존재를 나타냄 동사	I run
보어 Complement	문장의 주체에 대한 서술이나 분상 수제와 동격인 것을 나타냄 / 명사, 대명사, 형용사	I am a student (동격) I am happy (서술)
목적어 Object –을, –를	문장의 동사가 하는 행동의 목적이 되는 것을 의미 / 명사, 대명사	I kick a ball
이외에 간접목적어(Indirect Object) –에게, 직접목적어(Direct Object) –을, 목적보어(Object Complement) 등이 있음		

앞으로는 문장의 형식을 표현할 때 주어는 S, 동사는 V, 보어는 C, 목적어는 O, 간접목적어는 IO, 직접목적어는 DO, 목적보어는 OC로 쓰자.

1형식 : 주어와 동사만으로 문장이 되어 의사전달이 되는 형식

주어 (S) + 동사(V)(다른 어떤 것도 필요하지 않아 완전자동사라고 함)

Ex) I run fast 나는 빨리 달린다.

부사(문장의 구성요소에 들어가지 않음)

1형식 문장 중 시험에 자주 출제되는 문제는 장소를 나타내는 부사구가 앞에 나오면 주어동사가 도치된다는 원칙을 가진 문제가 있다.

Ex) On the hill, stands a horse 다음 문장을 보자. 이 문장은 언뜻 보기에는 틀려 보인다. 주어와 동사의 위치가 바뀌었기 때문이다. 하지만 장소부사구인 on the hill이라는 구가 앞으로 나오면서 주어동사가 도치된다는 원칙에 잘 맞게 문장을 구성한 것으로 맞는 문장이 된다.

절(Clause)과 구(Phrase)

이렇게 기억하자!

2개 이상의 단어가 묶여 있으면 구와 절이 될 수 있는데 절은 주어와 동사의 관계가 있는 것이고 구는 주어와 동사의 관계가 없는 것이다.

Ex) When it rains 비가 오면 (절)

On the hill 언덕 위에 (구)

2형식 : 의사전달을 위해 동사와 함께 보어(주어에 대한 서술이나, 주어와 같은(동격)을 나타내주는 문장성분)를 사용하여 의사전달을 하는 형식. 보어를 취해야 하기 때문에 불완전 자동사라고 함

주어(S) + 동사(V) + 보어(C)

보어는 두 가지 품사로 구성된다. 명사(동격), 형용사(서술)

Ex) I am a boy 나는 소년입니다.

명사(동격, I 가 a boy이라는 말)

I am beautiful 나는 아름답습니다.

형용사(서술, 나의 상태를 서술해주는 beautiful이라는 형용사를 씀)

2형식 동사 중 다음과 같은 동사는 외우는 것이 좋다.

모든 be 동사(am(과거 : was), is(was), are(were)), become(되다), go(되다) run(되다), remain(남다), keep(남다) continue(계속되다), feel(느끼다), sound(들리다), smell(냄새 맡다), taste(맛보다), look(보다).

그러니까 이런 동사 뒤에는 **형용사**나 **명사**가 올 것이라는 것을 바로 알 수 있게 될 것이다. 토익시험에서 이런 동사 뒤에 빈칸이 온다면 어떠한 품사가 와야 하는지는 더 이상 고민하지 않아도 될 것 같다.

3형식 : 문장에 동사의 목적이 되는 목적어가 첨가되는 문장 형식, 보통 문장의 해석이 '무엇이 무엇을 무엇하다' 의 식으로 된다.

※ She feel happy 문장의 해석은 '그녀는 행복을 느꼈다' 로 해석되어 3형식처럼 보이지만 실제로는 2형식의 문장이다. 그리고 실제로 정확한 해석은 '그녀는 행복하게 느꼈다' 이다. 1, 2형식과 과는 다르게 3형식 문장부터 달라지는 가장 큰 차이점은 목적어를 반드시 가진다는 것이다. 그래서 3형식 동사부터는 동사의 이름도 타동사라고 불린다(1, 2형식의 동사는 완전, 불완전 자동사라고 부른다).

주어(S) + 동사(V) + 목적어(O)

Ex) I kick a ball 내가 볼을 찬다.

명사(목적어) 볼을

3형식 동사를 쓸 때 한국어적인 생각으로 문장을 만들게 되면 동사의 쓰임을 잘못 이해하게 되어 영어적인 표현방식을 무너트리는 경우가 생긴다.

다음을 보자.

Ka-in married with Jo-Kwun.

이 문장은 맞는 표현일까요? 정답은 X.

영어의 표현에서 원래의 3형식 동사는 전치사를 취하지 않고 목적어를 가지게 된다. 따라서 이 문장은 Ka-in married Jo-Kwun.이라고 해야 맞는 문장이 된다. 이렇게 혼돈하기 쉬운 3형식 동사가 꽤 많고 이러한 동사는 기억해야만 한다.

다음은 전치사가 들어가지 않고 바로 쓰여야 하는 혼돈하기 쉬운 동사의 모임이다. (암기필요!)

marry(결혼), resemble(닮다), accompany(동반하다), enter(들어가다), approach(접근하다), mention(언급하다), discuss(토론하다), answer(답했다)

4형식 : 문장에 직접적인 목적어가 되는 직접목적어와 간접적인 목적어가 되는 간접 목적어가 있는 문장으로 보통 ~에게(간접목적어) ~을(직접목적어) 이라는 형태로 해석되는 문장을 일컫는다. 4형식 동사는 수여동사가 가장 많이 쓰인다.

※ 수여동사에는 give(주다), offer(제공하다), Lend(빌려주다), teach(가르치다), send(보내다), make(만들다), buy(사다), ask(묻다), inquire(묻다) 등의 동사가 있다.

주어(S) + 동사(V) + 간접목적어(I.O) + 직접목적어(D.O)

주어(S) + 동사(V) + 직접목적어(D.O) + 전치사 + 간접목적어(I.O)

Ex) I gave him a present.

내가 그에게 선물을 주었다.

I gave a present to him.

내가 선물을 그에게 주었다.

He make this cake for you.

그가 너를 위해 이 케익을 만들어 주었다.

Sam asked a serious question of me.

Sam이 나에게 질문 한가지를 했다.

동사마다 직접 · 간접 목적어의 순서를 바꾸게 될 때 들어가는 전치사가 다를 수 있는데 give, offer, lend는 전치사 to를 가져오고, make, buy 등은 for를, ask, inquire 등은 of를 가져오게 된다.

5형식 : 3형식의 문장에 목적어를 서술하는 형용사나 목적어와 같은 (동격) 명사가 들어가는 문장을 일컫는다. 5형식 동사는 이외에 목적격 보어로 분사, to 부정사, 동사원형을 취할 수 있다.

주어(S) + 동사(V) + 목적어(O) + 목적보어(O.C)

Ex) Sam called him the big guy(명사) 샘은 그를 큰사람이라고 불렀다.

그를 큰사람으로

People make him happy(형용사) 사람들은 그를 행복하게 만들었다.

그를 행복하게

I force him to do that(to 부정사) 나는 그가 그것을 하도록 강요했다.

그가 하도록 (him과 to do의 관계는 능동의 관계임)

I made my work done by him(분사) 내가 내 숙제를 그가 하도록 했다.

나의 숙제가 그에 의해 되도록 (수동의 관계)

I made him do that (원형) 나는 그가 그것을 하도록 만들었다.

그가 하도록 (능동의 관계)

5형식 문장에서는 동사에 사역동사(Let, have, make, bid)나 지각동사(see, watch, look at, hear, listen to, feel, notice)가 들어가면 **원형 부정사를 목적격 보어로 채택할 수** 있게 된다. (정말 중요함!!)

지각동사의 경우에는 목적어와 목적 보어의 관계가 능동일 때 진행의 의미를 나타내기 위해 ing(현재분사)가 가능하다라는 것도 알아 두어야 한다.

I saw him working in the factory.

나는 그가 공장에서 일하고 있는 것을 보았다.

과제

지금까지 배운 문장의 형식을 이용하여 각각의 형식마다 문장 10개씩 영작하기.

단어장 만들기

실전 문제

※ 다음 문장을 보고 틀린 부분을 골라 내시오.

1. Please don't force me read this.
2. Simpson was very tired so he made her to do all his work.
3. Sometime I had my work to do by my brother.
4. She married with a good looking man.
5. He resembles with his father.

※ 다음 빈칸에 알맞은 말을 고르시오.

6. We will let you __________ when we know the truth.

   a) To know b) know
   c) knowing d) known

7. In Mt Hana, _______ __________ there.

   a) a angry lion live b) live a angry lion
   c) living lion d) live lion

8. I always feel ________ when I eat that food.

   a) Happily b) Happy
   c) Happiness d) hope

글쓰기를 위한 팁

장문의 복잡한 말들을 읽다 보면 무슨 말을 하는지 모르는 때가 많다. 한 문장이 3줄 4줄 이상 길어지고 결국 의미전달이 약해질 수 밖에 없다. 쉬운 문장을 통해 자신이 표현하고자 하는 말을 간단히 적는 습관이 필요하다. 익숙하지 않고 뜻 모르는 단어를 통해 어렵게 쓰지 말고 배운 형식을 통해 간단 간단하게 표현해보자.
문장의 형식을 이용해서 오늘은 1형식 문장만을 만들어보고 내일은 2형식 문장을 만들어보자. 작은 노트하나 준비해서 간단한 문장을 만들어 지인에게 보여주고 간단한 feedback에 귀 기울여 보는 것도 괜찮을 것 같다. 자 그럼 문방구 다시 한번 가야 할 것 같다.

03 명사

명사의 의미 : 세상 모든 것들의 이름을 말한다.

문장에서 명사의 역할 : 주어, 목적어, 보어가 된다.

명사의 종류

보통명사	집합명사	고유명사	추상명사	물질명사
셀 수 있는 명사		셀 수 없는 명사		
단, 복수 구별이 있고 단수에는 부정관사(a, an)가 붙어야 하고, 복수형이 가능하다. 많다 적다고 표현할 때는 many나 few로 수식한다.		셀 수 없어서 복수형이 없고 부정관사(a, an)가 올 수 없고 복수형이 불가능하다. 많다 적다를 표현할 때는 much나 little로 수식한다.		
이 세상의 셀 수 있는 모든 명사 ex) House, cat, pencil, banana, computer	집합이나 단체를 나타내는 모든 명사 ex) Family, Audience (The police , the jury 항상 The와 같이 쓰이고 무조건 복수)	항상 대문자로 시작한다. ex) Joseph, Korea, Australia, Samsung,,,	눈에 보이는 형태가 없고 생각이나 개념을 나타낸다. ex) Peace, love, children, truth	형태가 고정되어 있지 않은 물질을 나타낸다. ex) Water, air, flour, rice, wood, silver

불가산 명사를 세고 싶을 때는 단위를 이용하여 그 양이 얼마인지 표현해줄 수 있다.

Ex) a piece of cheese, a sheet of paper, a glass of cocktail, two slices of bread

집합명사는 집합명사(단수취급, 집합체 전체), 군집명사(복수, 구성원의 개개인 고려)로 나눌 수 있다.

Ex) My family is large, My family are all well.

단수, 복수

먼저 단수, 복수가 무엇인지 알아야 할 것 같다. 단수는 하나의 물체를 이야기하고 복수는 두 가지 이상의 물체를 말한다는 것이다. 그런데 여기서 문제는 단수는 그냥 단어를 쓰지만 복수는 단어 뒤에 –s, –es, –ies, –ves가 붙어 단어를 표시하게 된다.

복수는 단어 끝에 s, es, ies, ves를 붙이게 된다.

단수명사를 복수명사로 만드는 법과 예제(여기에 제시된 단어는 반드시 외우자!!)

원칙	예제	예외
어미에 –s 를 붙인다.	book – books, tree – trees, girl – girls	
어미가 –s, –ss, –z, –sh, –x, –ch로 끝나면 –es를 붙인다.	bus – buses, miss – misses, box – boxes, wash – washes, match – matches, dish – dishes	
자음 + y로 끝나는 말은 y를 i로 고치고 –es를 붙인다.	city – cities, lady – ladies	
모음 + y로 끝나는 말은 그대로 –s를 붙인다.	boy – boys, monkey – monkeys	
자음 + o로 끝나는 말은 –es를 붙인다.	do – does, go – goes, tomato – tomatoes, hero – heroes	piano – pianos, photo – photos, radio – radios
어미가 f, fe로 끝나면 v로 고치고 –es를 붙인다.	knife – knives, wife – wives, wolf – wolves	roof – roofs, safe – safes

셀 수 있는 명사와 셀 수 없는 명사

위에서 말한 것처럼 명사의 종류는 보통명사, 집합명사, 고유명사, 추상명사, 물질명사로 나눈다. 여기에서 보통과 집합명사는 셀 수 있고 고유, 물질, 추상명사는 셀 수 없다. 이 말은 고유, 물질, 추상명사는 위의 복수명사로 만드는 원칙에 적용되지 않는다는 의미이기도 하다. 여기서 다시 한번 이 부분을 강조하는 이유는 이 부분이 시험에 자주 나오기 때문이고 영어의 말하기에서도 발음에 변화를 가져오기 때문이다.

그런데 정작 시험에 나오는 단어는 위에서 말해진 고유, 물질, 추상명사보다 다음에 제시되는 단어들이 더 많은 확률을 가지고 있다.

다음에 제시되는 단어들은 반드시 암기하고 넘어가자

Advice(충고), attention(주의), behavior(행동), confidence(신뢰), equipment(장비, 도구), evidence(증거), health(건강), information(정보), influenza(독감), money(돈), news(보도), oil(기름), pollution(오염), time(시간), weather(날씨),

학문 학과명은 복수의 형태를 가지지만 단수 취급한다.

ex) mathematics 수학, economics 경제학, statistics 통계학, politics 정치학.

machine(기계)은 단 복수 가능, machinery(기계류)는 셀 수 없는 명사이고,

이처럼 -류가 붙는 명사는 모두 셀 수 없다.

ex) jewelry(보석류), stationery(문구류)

셀 수 없는 명사를 암기해야 하는 중요한 이유

1) 항상 단수로 취급하고 복수형이 가능하지 않다.
   단위로 나타낼 때는 가능
   ex) two glasses of water / 복수로 나타낼 때도 여전히 단수를 쓴다는 사실
2) 부정관사 올 수 없고
3) 수를 나타내는 수식어인 many, a few, few로 수식할 수 없다.
4) 이러한 명사가 주어가 될 때는 같이 오게 되는 동사는 항상 단수동사만을 쓰게 된다.

동사의 단 · 복수 형태

	Be 동사	일반동사
단수	Am, Is (was)	주어가 단수일 때 동사 끝에 s, es를 붙인다.
복수	Are (were)	동사 원래의 형태를 씀

이 부분이 이해가 잘 되지 않더라도 너무 걱정하지 말자. 다음 장에서 나오는 수의 일치 부분을 공부하고 나면 더욱 이해가 쉬울 것이다!!

분화복수

단수와 복수가 되면 같은 단어 일지라도 뜻이 달라지는 단어들이 있다. 이를 분화복수라고 한다. 자 다음을 자세히 읽어 보자.

Ex) [advice 충고, 조언 / advices 보고] [통보, arm 팔 / arms 무기] [color 색깔 / colors 국기, 군기] [force 힘 작용 / forces 군대] [good 이익 / goods 상품] [letter 문자 / letters 문학, 증서] [premise 전제 / premises 시설 내] [saving 절약 / savings 저축] [time 때 / times 시대]

Ex) I think saving is very important.
나는 저축이 매우 중요하다고 생각한다.
I have a savings account.
나는 저축 통장을 가지고 있다.

항상 복수로 쓰는 명사

짝을 이루는 명사는 반드시 복수로 쓰고 복수 취급하지만 셀 수 없어 단위(a piece of)를 사용하게 된다.

Ex) a pair of glasses(안경), a pair of pants(바지)

합성명사

합성명사는 두 개 이상의 명사가 모여 하나의 명사가 되는 경우

Ex) tooth+paste=toothpaste(치약), bed+room=bedroom(침실),
movie star (영화배우)

앞의 명사가 뒤의 명사를 꾸며 주는 형용사의 역할을 하기 때문에 앞의 명사는 항상 단수로 쓰고 복수를 표현할 때는 뒤의 명사만 복수로 쓰게 된다.

Ex) movie stars, shoe stores

과제

앞에서 외운 것들을 친구들과 점검하는 시간을 가져 봅시다.

단어장 정리

실전 문제

※ 다음 빈칸에 들어갈 알맞은 말을 고르시오.

1. Sam desperately needs __________ for his last decision.

a) Information　　b) Informations
c) A information　　d) The information

2. When you go abroad for study, you need to open _______ account.

a) Saving　　b) Savings
c) A saving　　d) The savings

3. Why do you need so much these things?

I need many kinds of ___________ to get this job done.

a) Equipments　　b) The equipment
c) Equipment　　d) Some equipment

※ 다음의 문장에서 잘못된 부분을 찾아내시오.

4. It is a well known fact that people cannot live without water for more than a few day.

5. I know two well known movies stars in Korea.

글쓰기를 위한 팁

명사는 주어와 목적어 그리고 보어를 구성하는 매우 중요한 부분이다. 그래서 문장을 만들 때 그 선택에 있어 매우 중요하고 가장 핵심이 된다고 하겠다. 주어를 무엇으로 시작하려는 것인가에 대해 고민하고 문장의 핵심을 표현해보자. 위에서 언급된 간략한 표현을 위해서 수동태적인 표현보다는 능동태적인 표현을 통해 조금 더 직접적이고 간략한 표현을 이끌어내도록 하자. 이를 위해 내가 하려고 하는 말의 가장 주체가 누구인지 반드시 읽어 내고 문장에 옮기도록 하여야 할 것이다. 글쓰기를 오래하고 자신의 의사전달이 성숙되게 되면 저절로 수동태 적인 표현을 통해 은유적이고 강조적인 표현이 가능해질 수 있음을 명심하자.

04 수의 일치

시험에 많이 출제되는 부분이기도 하고 실생활에서 많이 사용되기도 한다. 완전한 암기를 통한 이해를 필요로 한다.

단수 주어는 단수동사를 받고 복수주어는 복수동사를 받는다

Ex) This cat is cute!!! 이 고양이는 귀엽다.

Those cats are all cute!!! 저기에 고양이들은 다 귀엽다.

항상 단수 취급하는 주어

Every		body	
Some	+	one	다음에는 항상 단수동사를 쓴다.
Any		thing	
No			

Ex) Someone takes this matter too seriously.

셀 수 없는 명사

고유, 물질, 추상명사

Advice(충고), attention(주의), behavior(행동), confidence(신뢰), equipment(장비, 도구), evidence(증거), health(건강), information(정보), influenza(독감), money(돈), news(보도), oil(기름), pollution(오염), time(시간), weather(날씨)

Ex) Sometimes too much attention is not good for children.

진짜 주어가 무엇인지 파악하고 동사를 결정한다.

주어와 동사 사이의 동격이나 수식어가 있는 문장에서는 동격이나 수식어 상관없이 원래 주어를 기준으로 동사를 쓴다.

Ex) The man, one of my friends, is my best friends

상관접속사인 Neither A nor B // Either A or B의 문장에서는 주어는 B이고 동사는 B에 일치시킨다.

Ex) Either they or Sam has a solution for that matter.

주의해야 할 주어들

1) A number of 복수명사는 복수동사를 취하고
The number of 복수명사는 단수동사를 취한다.
Ex) A number of students are doing this job today.
The number of students is decreasing

2) 시간, 거리 가격 무게의 복수명사는 단수동사를 쓴다.
Ex) Three meters of this wood is too long for this room.

3) 부분 또는 전체를 나타내는 표현 : 분수(Three – fourths of), 퍼센트(percent of), 나머지(the rest of) 등에서 전치사 뒤의 명사에 동사의 수를 일치시킨다
Ex) 60 percent of this land is under the construction.

4) 전체나 시리즈 또는 묶음(a total of, a serious of, a bunch of, a box of)을 나타내는 표현에서는 복수명사 뒤에 단수동사를 가져온다.
Ex) A serious of those book is on sale.

5) One of 복수명사의 주어는 단수동사만을 받는다.
Ex) One of students was late for school.

6) And나 both 로 연결된 주어는 항상 복수 취급한다.

Ex) Both Sumi and Chul su are my best friends

7) There is, There are에서 is와 are를 결정하는 것은 동사다음에 나오는 주어이다. There은 유도부사라고 하며 주어가 아니다.

Ex) There is one student in the class.

There are many students in the class.

8) 두 개의 관사가 사용되는 주어는 복수 취급하고 한 개의 관사가 사용되는 주어는 단수 취급한다.

Ex) A white and black dog was here yesterday.

A white and a black dog were here yesterday

과제

수의 일치에 해당하는 항목하나하나마다 한가지씩 자신만의 문장을 만들어 봅시다.

단어장 정리

실전 문제

※ 빈칸의 알맞은 말을 고르시오.

1. Fourteen kilometers of rainy roads __________ about an hour and half to drive.

a) Take
b) are to take
c) takes
d) taking

2. Almost 30 percent of problems ________ not from those incidents.

a) is
b) are
c) did
d) was

3. Are you going to the party?

I think so. Either I or Paul _______ going to get there to check it out.

a) am
b) are
c) is
d) were

※ 다음의 문장에서 잘못된 부분을 찾아내시오.

4. We need to move our house, because ours are too small for us.

5. Both you and I has something in common.

6. What I know about these matters are the company should do some more effort to us.

05 시제

동사는 문장에서 주체의 동작이나 상태를 나타내고 어느 시점에 이러한 것들이 행하여졌느냐에 따라서는 다른 형태를 가지게 되고 이를 시제라고 한다.

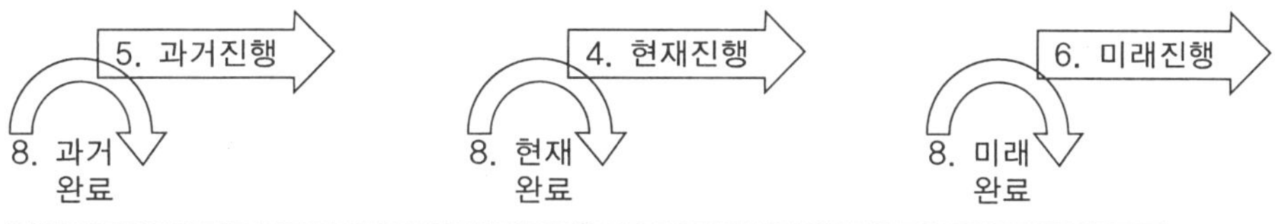

2. 과거	1. 현재	3. 미래
1) 역사적 사실	1) 현재의 상태, 사실	1) will
2) 과거의 사실, 상태, 습관, 경험	2) 변하지 않는 진리	2) be going to
3) 과거를 나타내는 단어나 부사구와 함께	3) 반복적 행동	3) 현재 진행형+미래시제
	4) 현재시제가 미래시제대신 a. 왕래발착 b. 시간, 조건부사절	

시제를 공부할 때 학생들이 반드시 염두해두어야 하는 것은 시제는 단순히 어느 시점이라는 것 이외에도 여러 가지 사항을 나타낼 수 있으며 이러한 사실에 대해서 반드시 기억하여야 한다는 것이다. 이번 장에서는 조금은 책을 읽듯이 문장을 읽어주고 '아 이런 시제는 이런 때 이렇게 쓰는구나' 라고 이해해주었음 한다.

현재

먼저 현재시제는 현재의 상태를 나타낸다. 이 말은 현재의 사실을 표현한다는 말이다. 즉 I am a student라는 말은 현재 나는 학생이라는 직업을 가지고 있다는 말이다.

두 번째로 현재시제는 변하지 않는 진리 즉 불변의 진리를 나타내는데 사용한다. The sun rises from the east라는 말은 태양은 동쪽에서 뜬다는 말로 태양이 어느 쪽에서 지고 어느 쪽에서 진다는 말은 변하는 사실이 아닌 진리라는 말이다.

세 번째로 현재시제는 반복적인 행동을 나타낼 때 쓰인다. 최근에 계속적으로 반복되는 행동들을 나타낼 때 쓰이게 되는데 가령 '나는 아침에 일어나면 간단한 운동을 한다' 라는 문장을 표현하기 위해서는 I do simple exercise when I wake up이라고 표현할 수 있다는 말이다.

네 번째로 현재시제는 일부의 표현에 있어 미래시제를 대신하는 경우가 있는데 기차역, 비행기, 버스의 출발이나 도착 그리고 항상 왕래하는 길에 관한 표현은 현재시제가 미래 시제를 대신하게 된다. 예를 들어 '기차가 7시 30분에 출발할 것이다' 라는 표현은 The train will leave at 7:30라고 표현하지 않고 The train leaves at 7:30이라고 표현한다.

다섯 번째로 시간조건 부사절에서는 현재시제가 미래시제를 대신하게 된다. 한가지 조건이 만족되면 다른 한가지 조건이 이루어진다는 말을 표현할 때 첫 번째 만족되는 조건에서 현재시제를 두 번째 만족되는 조건에서 미래시제를 쓴다는 말이다. 예를 들어 If it rains tomorrow, we will not(won' t)go camping 이라는 문장은 '내일 비가오면 소풍을 가지 않는다' 는 말이고 비가 오는 것도 미래이고 소풍을 가는 것도 미래이지만 먼저 만족되어야 하는 조건이 비가 온다는 조건은 미래의 일임에도 현재시제를 통해 표현하고 나머지 표현은 미래시제를 통해 표현하고 있음을 알 수 있다. 또한 Let' s see what happen과 같은 문장은 무슨 일이 일어나는지 지켜보자는 말이다. 여기서 일이 일어나는 것은 분명이 미래이지만 현재시제를 통해 미래의 시제를 표현하고 있음을 알 수 있다.

시험에 매우 자주 출제되고 이해에 있어 조금은 암기가 필요한 문장이다. 반드시 예문을 암기해서 이해하도록 하자.

과거

과거시제는 역사적 사실을 묘사할 때 쓰이게 된다.

ex) The 1988 Summer Olympics were an international multi-sport event celebrated in 1988 in Seoul, South Korea

또한 과거의 사실, 상태, 습관, 경험을 나타낼 때 쓰이게 된다. 특히 과거를 지칭하는 특정한 문구(last night, yesterday 등)들이 같이 나오게 되면 반드시 과거시제를 써주어야 한다는 사실을 잊지 말자.

ex) I ate Bul-Go-Gi last night.

과거의 불규칙적 습관을 나타낼 때는 Would를 사용하게 된다. 예를 들어 '나는 주말에 테니스를 치곤 했다' 라는 문장을 영작할 때는 'I would play tennis on the weekend' 라고 표현하게 된다.

미래

미래를 나타내는 표현은 크게 두 가지가 있는데 하나는 will을 써서 문장을 표현하고 단순한 미래, 강한 의지, 먼 미래 또는 지금 결정한 미래를 표현할 때 쓰게 된다.

예를 들이 'I will study harder' 라는 말은 '나는 지금부터 공부를 열심히 하겠다' 라고 하는 강한 의지나 지금 결정한 미래를 나타낼 때 쓸 수 있게 된다.

다른 한가지는 be going to인데 -할 예정이라는 표현 또는 앞으로 일어날 일이 자명하게 나타날 때 쓰이게 된다.

예를 들어 '오늘 6시에 그 사람을 만날 예정이다' 라고 표현할 때는 'I am going to meet him' 이라고 표현한다. 그리고 멀리서 먹구름이 몰려오는 것을 보고 '비가 오겠다' 고 말할 때도 'It is going to rain' 이라고 표현한다.

이외에도 현재진행형(be -ing)과 미래시제가 같이 문장에 쓰이게 되면 미래를 나타내는 말과 같은 표현이 된다는 것도 알아두자.

예를 들어 'I am playing tennis this Saturday' 라는 말은 '이번 주 토요일에 테니스를 칠 것이다' 라는 미래형을 표현하는 말이 된다.

현재진행형(be + 동사원형 ing)

현재진행형은 지금 현재 일어나고 있는 일을 표현할 때 쓰게 되는 표현이다. 이는 현재 시제와는 반드시 구분지어야 하는데 '나는 요즘 셰익스피어를 읽고 있어' 라는 말은 'I am reading Shakespeare' 라고 하지 않고 'I read Shakespeare' 라고 표현해야 한다. '나는 지금 셰익스피어를 읽고 있어' 라는 말이 바로 전자의 표현이 되는 것이다. 그리고 'now, at the moment' 와 같은 표현은 현재진행형의 시제와 같이 올 수 있다.

과거진행형(was or were + 동사원형 ing)

과거진행형은 과거에 일어나고 있었던 일을 표현할 때 쓰이게 된다. 'I was studying really hard that time' 이라는 말은 '나는 그때 정말 공부를 열심히 하고 있었다' 라는 말이 된다.

미래진행형(will 동사원형 +ing)

'나는 내일 이 시간에 열심히 공부하고 있을 거야' 라고 하는 문장은 'I will be studying at this time tomorrow' 라고 표현한다.

현재완료(have (has) + P.P) *P.P는 과거완료를 나타낸다

현재완료는 일단 ① 경험(해보았던 것들), ② 결과(과거의 행동으로 현재 상태의 변화), ③ 완료(현재 일이 끝난 상황), ④ 진행(과거의 일이 여전히 진행되고 있는 상황)을 나타낼 때 사용하게 된다.

먼저 이미 해보았던 것들을 나타낼 때 현재완료형을 사용하게 된다. 예를 들어 '너 이탈리아에 가봤니?' 라고 물을 때는 현재완료형을 써서 표현할 수 있다. 'Have you been Italy?'

결과를 나타낸다는 말은 과거의 행동으로 일어난 일로 인해 현재 상태가 달라진 것을 의미한다. 예를 들어 'She has gone to the U.S.A' 라고 한다면 그녀는 과거에 미국으로 갔고 지금 여기에 없다는 것을 의미한다.

현재 일이 마무리된 상태를 나타낼 때 현재완료시제를 사용하게 된다. 'I have just finished this work' 이라는 말은 '난 금방 이 일을 다 끝냈다' 는 말이다. 예문에서 보이듯이 이러한 문장에는 보통 just(이제 금방)나 already(이미) 등의 부사가 같이 오게 된다.

자, 다음 문장을 영작 또는 말한다고 가정해보자.

'나는 영어공부를 1999년 이후로 계속 해오고 있다' 라는 문장은 흔히 'I have been studying English since 1999' 라고 영작하기 쉬울 것 같다. 현재완료가 과거에서 시작되어 현재까지 계속된다고 배웠고, 현재진행은 지금 일어나고 있는 일을 묘사할 때 쓰니까 말이다. 하지만 이건 틀린 영작이 된다. 다시 한번 말씀 드리고 싶은 것은 현재진행은 지금 현재진행되고 있는 일을 나타낼 때 쓰이게 된다. 위의 문장을 정확하게 해석한다면 난 1999년부터 영어공부를 해오고 있고 지금 내가 말하는 순간에도 영어공부를 하고 있다는 말이 된다. 따라서 정확한 영문장의 표현은 'I have studied English since 1999' 라고 쓰고 말해야 한다.

현재시제를 정확하게 이해했다면 왜 현재완료시제만으로도 위의 표현이 가능한지를 잘 알 수 있을 것이다. 현재시제는 습관이나 반복적인 사실을 나타낼 수 있으니까!!!

과거완료(had + P.P)

과거완료는 현재완료의 과거버전이다. 말 그대로 현재완료가 경험, 결과, 완료, 진행을 나타내었다면 과거완료는 과거의 어느 시점이나 일정 기간 동안의 경험, 결과, 완료, 계속을 나타내는 말이나 문장에 쓰일 수 있게 된다. 'I had finished that work' 라는 말은 '나는 과거에 그 일을 끝낸 상태였다' 라는 의미이다. 과거완료는 현재완료가 가진 기능 이외에 대과거를 나타낼 때 쓰이게 된다. 이 말은 과거보다 더 과거를 나타낼 때 이 시제를 써서 표현하면 된다.

미래완료(will have + P.P)

미래완료의 핵심은 그 문장의 해석이다. 미래완료를 쓴 문장의 해석은 '그때가 되면 그것은 ~이 되어 있을 것이다' 로 해석될 수 있다. 물론 현재 완료의 4가지 용법이 여기서도 적용될 수 있다는 사실 명심하자.

과제

각 시제를 노트에 나열하고 그 특징에 대해서 정리하고 난 후 각 시제마다의 다양한 특징별로 한 문장씩 만들어 봅시다.

단어장 정리

실전 문제

※ 다음 문장을 읽고 어색한 부분을 바르게 고쳐 문장을 다시 쓰시오.

1. They have met Mr. Clark yesterday.

____

2. My family has moved to Seoul three years ago.

____

3. When have you been to so many cities in Korea?

____

4. Do you have seen Brad and Jennifer recently?

____

※ 다음 문장을 읽고 괄호 안의 주어진 단어를 바르게 고쳐 문장을 다시 쓰시오. (단, 모든 문장은 현재 시제임)

5. Mrs. Doe (mixs, mixes) flour with eggs and milk.

____

6. He (don't clean, doesn't clean) his room on weekdays.

____

7. (Do, Does) your brothers help around the house?

____

8. She (doesn't play, isn't play) any computer games at all.

____

※ 주어진 문장을 괄호 안의 지시대로 고쳐 다시 쓰시오.

9. They make expensive cars in their company.

(부정문) : ______________________________

(의문문) : ______________________________

※ 다음 괄호 안의 단어 중 바른 것을 골라 문장을 완성하여 다시 쓰시오.

10. He (is having, is hasing) a fun time with his friends.

____

11. I (am not, not) playing computer games.

____

※ 주어진 한글 뜻에 맞게 영작하시오.

12. 그의 할아버지는 작년 겨울부터 줄곧 아프십니다. (last winter, ill)

____

13. 그녀는 매일 밤 열한 시에 잠자리에 듭니다.

____

14. 나는 매일 아침 공원에서 조깅을 합니다.

____

15. 당신은 지금 어디에 가고 있습니까? (where, go)

____

16. 그들은 요즘 잘 지내고 있습니까? (how, these days)

____

※ 괄호 안의 주어진 단어를 이용하여 빈칸에 바른 표현을 넣어 문장을 다시 쓰시오.

17. A : You look tired.

B : Yes. I __________ on this project for six hours. (work)

18. A : Are you hungry?

B : Yes. I __________ anything since this morning. (eat)

06 조동사

조동사는 말 그대로 동사를 보조해주는 동사이다. 동사 자체로는 나타낼 수 없는 것들 즉 미래, 가능성, 허락, 능력, 추측, 당연, 의무 등을 나타내고자 할 때 동사를 보조하여 문장의 표현력을 강화한다고 생각하면 된다. 그리고 문장의 주된 동사가 be 동사의 경우(I am a boy)를 제외하고는 의문문이나 부정문을 만드는 경우와 위에서 말해진 경우들을 표현할 때 그리고 의문문이나 부정문을 표현해주고자 할 때 반드시 조동사를 써서 표현해야 한다. 그리고 조동사 뒤에는 반드시 동사원형이 와야 한다. 말이 어렵다고 이제 구체적으로 한번 살펴보자.

조동사의 주요 기능 : 의문문, 부정문 만들기

조동사의 주요 기능은 의문문과 부정문을 만들 때 반드시 필요하다. Be 동사의 경우 be 동사는 조동사의 기능을 대신하여 쓴다. 먼저 다음 예문을 보자.

You are happy의 의문문은 Are you happy?이다. 여기서 be 동사인 are는 문장의 맨 앞으로 나가면서 의문문을 만들고 이때 are는 문장의 조동사의 기능을 겸하게 된다.

역시 'You are happy' 의 부정문은 'You are not happy' 가 되고 이때 be 동사인 'are' 은 'not' 을 취하면서 문장의 조동사의 기본 기능을 수행하게 된다.

그런데 우리가 말하고 쓰는 문장에는 be 동사 외에 많은 동사들이 일반동사(eat, kick,,,)가 있다. 이러한 동사는 의문문을 만들 때 do 동사를 이용해서 의문문과 부정문을 만들어주게 되는데 이 말은 do 동사가 문장의 조동사의 역할을 하게 된다는 말이다.

'You eat dinner' 의 의문문은 be 동사의 의문문처럼 그냥 주어동사의 위치만 바꾸어수는 것이 아니라 do 동사를 이용해서 의문문과 부정문을 만든다. 즉 'Do you eat dinner?' 이나 'You don't eat dinner' 이라고 표현해주어야 한다. (여기서 주의할 것은 주어가 삼인칭 단수이면서 동사가 현재형일 경우 반드시 does를 써주어야 하고 과거시제일 경우에는 'did' 를 써주어야 한다.

자! 이제 조동사를 통해 의문문을 만드는 경우를 생각해보자. 'I will do it' 이라는 문장을 생각해보자. 이 문장의 의문문은? 간단하게 조동사와 주어의 위치만 바꾸어주면 된다. 그래서 'Will I do it?' 이 된다. 부정문은 'I will not do it.' 이 된다.

Can, Could, Be able to

조동사에 대한 이해를 시작할 때 보통 can부터 시작하게 된다. 왜냐하면 can이 나타내는 것이 시제를 설명할 때 현재 시제를 설명하고 다른 시제를 거기에 비추어 설명하는 것처럼 can의 기능이 다른 조동사의 기능을 이해하는데 중요하기 때문이다.

먼저 Can은 가능성, 능력, 허락, 추측을 표현하고자 할 때 사용된다는 것을 예문과 함께 암기하도록 하자. (매우 중요!!!)

Can	가능성	능력	I Can do it!
		허락	Can you do it?
		추측	It can be true

과거의 추측은 : cannot have p.p : She cannot have done such a thing 그녀는 그러한 일을 했을 리가 없다.

Could	Can의 과거형	I could do it!!	내가 할 수 있었다.
	공손한 표현	Could you do me a favor?	부탁 하나 해도 될까요?
	일반적인 능력	He could speak three different languages.	그는 삼개 국어를 할 수 있다(일반적인 표현을 구사할 수 있다)
	지각동사와 함께 쓰여서 불확실한 추측을 나타내기도 한다.	I could smell Bul go ki	불고기 냄새가 나는 것 같은데…

Be able to	현재 상황을 잘 알고 있을 때	He is unable to race tomorrow, due to his bad injury.	부상으로 인해 그는 내일 경기를 할 수 없다.
	조동사가 겹칠 때	I will be able to do this.	나는 이것을 할 수 있을 것이다. (미래에)

May, Might

May는 허가와 추측(불확실)을 그리고 정말 공손한 표현을 나타낼 때 사용한다.

May	허가	May I use this phone?	이 전화 사용해도 될까요?
	추측	He may meet them.	그는 그들을 만날지도 모른다.
	공손한 표현	May I help you?	제가 도와드릴까요?
	기원	May god bless you!!	하나님의 가호가 있기를!!

Might는 may의 과거형으로 위의 표현으로 쓰일 수 있는데 허가에 있어서는 잘 쓰이지 않고 추측에 있어 may보다 더 불확실한 추측을 나타낼 때 쓰이고 기원의 표현에도 사용될 수 있다.

May와 Might의 경우 관용적 표현을 잘 기억해야 한다.

1. may well 동사원형 : -하는 것이 당연하다.

 You may well be good at this.

 당신이 이것에 대해서 잘하는 것은 당연하다.

2. may as well 동사원형 : -하는 것이 낫다.

 She may as well quit this job.

 그녀는 이 직업을 그만두는 것이 낫다.

3. might as well a as b : b 하는 것 보다 a 하는 것이 낫다.

 You might as well study harder as quit school.

Will, Would, Shall

Will	강한의지	I will be a teacher!!	나는 선생님이 될 거야!!
	지금결정	I will help mom!	엄마를 도와야겠다!
	먼미래	I will study	공부할거야

Be going to : 역시 미래를 표현하는 조동사이다. 하지만 will과는 다르게 예정된 미래나 가까운 미래를 표현할 때 쓰이는 것으로 실생활에서는 이 표현이 조금 더 많이 쓰인다고 할 수 있을 것이다.

Ex) I am going to watch a movie tonight

오늘 영화 보러 갈 예정이야.

Would	과거의 습관적 행동	I would go there.	거기에 가곤 했다.
	공손한 표현	Would you like to have more coffee?	커피 좀 더 드시겠습니까?
	소망에 관한 표현	If you would go there, you better be hurry.	거기에 가기를 원한다면 좀더 서둘러라.

관용적 표현 : Would rather A than B : B 하느니 A 하는 것이 낫다.

I would rather go there than sleep in here.

거기에 가느니 차라리 여기에서 잠을 자는 것이 나을 것 같다.

Must, Have to, Should, Ought to, Had better

Must = Have to	의무. 필요 강한 표현, -해야 한다	I must try harder.	난 더 열심히 해야만 해.
	강한 추측	He must be gay!	그는 동성애자임이 틀림없어.

must와 have to는 같은 표현이지만 부정형으로 표현되면 둘의 표현에 상당한 차이가 발생된다. Must not = 절대 -하면 안 된다. don't have to : 할 필요는 없다. 이러한 이유로 쓰임에 매우 주의가 요구된다. 그리고 must는 부정형이 없어서 must

의 과거형에 부정형은 didn' t have to로 표현해야만 하는데 여기서 didn' t have to가 must의 과거부정형인지 (틀림없이 -하면 안되었었다) have to의 과거부정형인지(-할 필요는 없었었다)를 밝혀낼 필요가 경우가 발생하는데 이것은 문장의 흐름에서 파악될 수 있을 것이라고 생각된다.

Should	의무, 당연(-해야 한다)	We should try harder.	우리는 더 열심히 해야 한다.
	추측, 가능성(-일 것이다. -하게 될 것이다)	They should be there.	그들은 거기에 도착했을 것이다. (예정대로 라면..)

위의 must에서 쓰였던 의무, 필요와 should의 의무, 당연은 비슷한 표현이다. 여기서 조금은 혼란이 올 수 있을 것 같은데, should는 그렇게 되는 것이 옳다라는 것이고 must는 반드시 그렇게 되어야 한다로 인식하는 것이 옳겠다. 그러니까 must는 강제성이 조금 있고 should는 원래 우리가 해야 할 일이니까 해야 한다는 의미로 해석하는 것이 맞을 것이다.

Ought to

역시 의무나 당연을 나타내는 말로 should와 같은 표현, 여기서 주의할 것은 ought to의 부정형은 ought not to가 된다는 것을 잊지 말자.

This ought not to be here. 이것은 여기에 있어서는 안 된다.

Had better

Had better은 약간의 협박성(?) 발언이다. 그렇지만 must 보다는 약하고 should 보다는 조금 더 강한 표현으로 보면 될 것이다. 중요한 것은 have better이라는 표현은 없다는 것, 그리고 had better 다음은 항상 동사원형을 쓴다는 것 기억하자.

Used to, Be used to, need

Used to는 과거에는 정규적으로 했던 행동들이었으나 지금은 하지 않는 행동에 대해 표현할 때 쓰이게 된다. 과거형은 과거의 행동만을 나타내고 현재에는 무엇을 하는지 파악하지 못하지만 used to는 이러한 표현을 가능하게 해준다.

I was a student = 나는 과거에 학생이었다(현재는 무엇인지 알 수 없다).

I used to be a student = 나는 과거에 학생이었지만 지금은 학생이 아니다.

여기서 한가지 주의해야 할 것은 used to 앞에 be 동사가 붙으면 전혀 다른 쓰임을 가져온다는 것도 알아 둘 필요가 있다. 다음 원칙과 예문들은 암기 될 때까지 충분한 학습이 필요하다.

Be used to + 명사(동명사) = ~에 익숙하다.

I am used to dormitory.

나는 기숙사에 익숙하다.

I am used to this kind of things.

나는 이런 일들에 익숙하다.

I am used to moving this kind of stuff.

나는 이런 종류의 물건들을 옮기는데 익숙하다.

Be used to + 동사 = ~하는데 사용된다.

This computer is used to calculate all our process.

이 컴퓨터는 우리의 모든 공정들을 계산하는데 이용된다.

Need는 동사로 알고 있지만 조동사로 사용될 때가 있다. 알아두자. 쓰임은 '~할 필요가 있다' 로 쓰인다.

We needn't do this.

우리는 이것을 할 필요가 없다.

조동사와 have + p.p

조동사와 have + p.p가 같이 쓰이게 되면 여러가지 특수한 의미를 지니게 되는데 대화 속에서 이러한 말들이 나오면 잘 알아듣기 힘들 수도 있어서 매우 중요하게 다루어야 하고 반드시 암기해야 하는 부분이기도 하다.

Must have p.p ~이었음에 틀림없을 것이다.

He must have been there.

그는 틀림없이 거기에 가봤을 것이다.

Cannot have p.p ~했을 리 없다.

He is such a nice boy, he cannot have done such a things.

그는 아주 친절한 사람이라, 그러한 일을 했을 리가 없다.

May have p.p ~이었을 런지도 모른다.

She may have worked for C.I.A.

그녀는 CIA에서 일했을는지도 모른다.

Should have p.p ~했어야 했는데 하지 않았다.

You should have studied Medicine.

너는 의학공부를 했어야 했는데…

Need not have p.p ~할 필요가 없는데 했다.

You need not have done this.

넌 이것을 할 필요가 없었는데 했구나.

과제

책을 읽고 난 후 각 조동사의 의미를 노트에 적어 봅시다. 그리고 각 조동사의 의미에 따른 자신만의 문장 한 문장씩 만들어 봅시다.

조동사의 관용구 3가지 기억나는 대로 노트에 적고 문장을 만들어봅시다.

난어상 성리

실전 문제

※ 다음 ( ) 안에 들어갈 알맞은 말을 고르시오.

1. She (could, will, would) open play the piano when she had free time.

2. (Will, Shall, May) I use your eraser?

※ 빈칸에 알맞은 말을 고르시오.

3. A: What should I do?

B: I think you should ____________ first.

a) have finished this job　　b) finishing

c) finished this job　　d) finish this job

4. A: Have you heard that she has just won lottery?

B: Mate! You ______________ with her.

a) should have broken　　b) need to break

c) would break　　d) could have broken

※ 다음 밑줄친 부분 중 어색한 부분을 찾아 바르게 고쳐 쓰시오.

5. General Manager decided to do those projects, he must suffered for a long time.

6. Because of recent incidents in security, the hotel needs to be adapted new policy for the future matter.

07 수동태

수동태를 공부하기 전에 반드시 알아야 할 것은 왜 수동태를 쓰는가에 대한 인식이다. 수동태는 원래는 목적어가 되었던 것을 주어의 자리에 놓으면서 문장의 원래 느낌과는 다른 표현을 할 수 있게 해주고 다른 요소의 강조를 통해 듣는 사람이 다른 부분에 대해 더 강하게 인식할 수 있게 하기 위함이다.

수동태는 먼저 3형식 이상의 문장이 수동태가 된다는 것 알아야 한다. 이는 수동태의 문장을 만들기 위해서는 반드시 목적어가 있어야 한다는 것이다. 그리고 동사의 형태는 be + p.p 형태로 바뀌어지고 주어는 문장의 끝에 by + 주어(목적격)으로 바뀌게 되고 be동사에서 전에 문장의 시제를 알 수 있게 된다.

I broke the glass → The glass was broken by me

위의 문장은 전형적인 수동태의 문장으로 목적어가 주어로 오고 동사의 형태가 변하고 주어가 목적격으로 변하면서 문장의 뒤로 갔음을 볼 수 있다.

수동태의 공부를 제대로 하기 위해서는 많은 암기가 필요한데, 여기서 중요하다고 생각되는 문장들을 나열하면서 문장을 설명해보도록 하겠다. 모든 문장에 대해 철저한 이해가 필요하므로 한 문장 한 문장 기억하면서 왜 그렇게 되는지에 대해서 완전히 익히도록 하자. 쉬운 게 없지만 못할 것도 없지!!!

일반적인 수동태

I kick the ball → The ball is kicked by me.

목적어가 명사절인 경우

It is said that they do that work. → They are said to do work (by people)
by people과 같이 일반적인 사람들이나 모두가 알고 있는 경우에는 생략가능하다.

It is said that they did that work. → They are said to have worked (by people)

위의 문장과 아래문장에서 that 절 이하의 시제가 다름을 알 수 있다. 두 번째 문장처럼 that 절의 시제가 한 시제 더 과거의 시제이면 that 절의 변형은 to have p.p (완료 부정사)가 와야 한다.

4형식의 수동태

두 가지의 수동태가 가능할 것이다. 왜나 하면 4형식의 문장은 두 가지의 목적어가 있기 때문이다. 그런데 2가지의 목적어를 가지고 무조건 다 수동태를 만들 수 있는 것은 아니다. 다음의 문장을 한번 보자.

I bought him a present. → A present was bought for him by me는 가능하지만 He was bought a present by me는 원래의 문장에서 말하려고 했던 의도와 너무 다르고 문장의 해석에서 느낄 수 있겠지만 말이 잘 안 되는 경향이 있어 이렇게 쓰지 않게 된다. 이러한 동사의 종류에는 buy, read, sell, send, write 등이 있다는 것 알아두자.

그리고 다음 문장도 한번 자세히 살펴 보자. He refused her to come in. -> She was refused to come in by him.은 가능하지만 To come in was refused her by him이란 문장은 말이 되지 않는다는 것 알 수 있을 것이다. 많은 학습서에 동사별로 이런 문장이 가능하다 하지 않다라는 것을 외우라고 하는 경우가 있는데 이러한 것은 전혀 필요가 없을 것 같다. 왜냐하면 문장이 잘못되어 있다는 것 그냥 해석해 봐도 알 수 있기 때문이다. 여기서 중요한 것은 문장의 구성에 있어 변형은 제한적일 수 있다는 것 알아두면 된다는 것이다.

5형식의 수동태 (매우 중요!!)

I made him happy → He was made happy by me.

I made him a doctor. → He was made a doctor by me.

앞의 문장의 형식을 설명하는 장에서 이미 말했던 것처럼 한문장 안에는 하나의 동사가 나와야 하는 것을 원칙으로 하는데 지각동사(see, hear, watch)나 사역동사(let, make, have, bid)의 동사가 문장의 중심동사로 오면 목적어와 목적보어의 관계가 능동일 때 원형부정사가 온다는 것 설명하였다. 그런데 이러한 문장의 수동태는 다시 to 부정사가 살아난다는 원칙을 설명하고자 한다.

I made him cry → He was made to cry by me.

I saw him do that → He was seen to do that by me.

He let me do it → I was allowed to do it by him.

수동태가 될 수 없는 동사

앞에서 말해진 것처럼 문장이 수동태가 되려면 목적어가 있어야 하고 목적어를 가지는 동사는 타동사 이므로 자동사는 목적어를 가지지 않음으로 수동태가 될 수 없다. 자동사를 다 암기할 수는 없겠지만 일반적으로 많이 쓰이는 자동사는 암기해두는 것이 문제를 푸는데 유리하고 문장의 이해력을 높일 수 있을 것이다.

수동태를 만들 수 없는 자동사 : appear, occur, come, rise, lie, fall…

여기서 한가지 또 기억해야 할 것은 타동사 중에도 수동태로 쓰지 않는 동사가 있다는 것이다. 다음의 동사는 수동태로 쓰지 않는 동사이다.

Have(가지다), cost, resemble, marry, hold

He resembles his father. → His father is resembled by him

(말이 안 된다는 거 알고 있을 것이다!!)

동사구의 수동태

동사 중에 전치사와의 결합을 통해서 다른 의미를 나타내는 동사가 있는데 이러한 동사는 항상 그 전치사와 같이 움직인다는 거 기억하자. 이런 동사는 주로 자동사가 많고 자동사와 전치사의 결합을 통해 목적어를 가지는 타동사의 역할을 하게 된다. 그러니까 수동태가 가능하게 된다.

They look into the incident → The incident is looked by them.

다음에 나오는 동사는 전치사와 같이 쓰이는 동사이다. 뜻 찾아 여러분의 단어장에 기록해놓고 반드시 외우도록 하자.

Deal with, depend on, look at, look into, rely on, listen to, account for, attend to.

동사구에는 전치사와의 결합 외에도 동사+명사+전치사, 또는 동사+부사+전치사의 결합을 통해 다른 의미를 나타내고는 하는데 여기서 그 몇 가지 소개하고자 한다.

I take care of him → He is taken care of me.

She pays attention to the movie → The movie is pay attention to by her.

She speaks well of him → He is well spoken of by her

자! 이제 수동태의 가장 어려운 부분인 관용구에 대해서 공부할 차례이다. 관용구는 반드시 외워야 하고 필수적으로 기억되고 문장으로 만들어질 수 있어야 한다. 아래에 제시된 수동태의 관용구 반드시 사전을 통해 뜻을 찾고 암기하고 문장으로 만들어보자. 관용구는 항상 수동태의 문장으로 쓰여야만 한다는 것 잊지 말자. 단어장!!!!

Be filled with, be covered with, be satisfied with, be delight with, be concerned with, be fed up with, be known as, be known for, be known by, be known to, be born, get married, be expected to, be exposed to, be composed of, be interested in, be engaged in, be worried about, be made of, be made from. Need to be p.p

그리고 이 책의 마지막 부분에 있는 불규칙 동사표는 반드시 한번 보고 모르는 단어는 반드시 정리하여 암기해야 한다.

과제

능동태와 수동태의 차이를 설명해 봅시다. 그리고 각각의 형태를 한 문장씩 만들어 봅니다. 5형식의 문장(사역동사를 이용)을 하나 만들고 난 후 수동태로 고쳐 봅시다.

수동태의 관용구 5가지를 외우고 난 후 문장을 만들어 봅시다.

단어장 정리

실전 문제

※ 괄호 안의 알맞은 단어를 골라 문장을 완성하여 다시 쓰시오.

1. My baby sister is (loving, loved) by everybody in the family.

____

2. The Pyramid was (build, built) by many people in Egypt.

____

3. These roses (was, were) planted by my grandmother last year.

____

※ 다음 문장을 읽고 어색한 표현을 바르게 고쳐 문장을 다시 쓰시오.

4. The cake was making by me and my mother together.

____

5. I was fed my dogs and cats every day.

____

6. These letters was written by my friends.

____

7. My sister was born ______ the little city in Ghana.

____

8. This fine wine was made ______ grapes grown in California.

____

9. We are very much interested ______ learning new things.

____

10. The TV wasn't turned ______. I really need a quiet place to study.

____

11. The room was filled ______ young boys and girls who don't know each other.

____

※ 다음 주어진 문장을 수동태 또는 능동태로 바꾸어 쓰고 그 후 괄호 안의 지시대로 다시 한번 바꾸어 쓰시오.

12. She can finish the work on time.

____

(의문문) ______________________________

13. I didn't do the homework yesterday.

____

(긍정문) ______________________________

※ 주어진 한글 뜻에 맞게 수동태 문장을 영어로 쓰시오.

14. 그 은행은 어제 어떤 남자들에 의해 도둑맞았습니다. (rob)

____

15. 그 일기는 그에 의해서 십년 동안 써져 왔습니다. (keep, written)

____

16. 그 잡지는 이곳에서 매우 잘 팔립니다. (here, sell)

____

08 준동사

준동사란 동사의 모양을 가지고 있지만 술어 동사(문장에서 주체의 동작이나 상태를 나타내는 동사)로 사용될 수 없는 동사를 이야기한다. 즉 동사의 모양을 가지지만 역할은 다른 품사의 것들을 하는 것을 말한다.

부정사는 명사, 형용사, 부사의 역할을, 동명사는 명사의 역할을, 그리고 분사는 형용사의 역할을 할 수 있다는 말이다. 이 말은 부정사는 주어, 목적어, 보어가 될 수 있다는 말이고 동명사도 주어, 목적어, 보어가 될 수 있다는 말이다. 분사는 형용사의 역할을 하기 때문에 형용사의 역할인 수식과 서술의 역할을 하게 되고 문장의 요소로는 보어의 역할을 할 수 있다.

준동사의 이해는 각 준동사의 역할에 따른 예문을 암기하고 추가적인 관용적 표현에 대해서 기억함으로써 학습을 마치게 된다.

형태는 To + 동사원형을 가지게 된다. 즉 'eat'는 '먹다'라는 동사이지만 이것을 to 부정사로 만들기 위해서는 to eat가 된다는 말이다.

명사적 용법

쓰임 : 명사적으로 쓰이기 때문에 주어, 목적어, 보어가 될 수 있다.

주어가 되는 경우 : To get there is not easy 거기에 가는 것은 쉽지 않다.

보통 문장의 주어가 너무 길게 되면 문장이 모호해지므로 문장의 주어는 짧게 가져가는 것이 좋고 이를 위해 가주어인 it을 넣어 주면서 문장을 바꾸어주기도 한다.

It is not easy to get there.

목적어가 되는 경우 : I want to meet him.

보어가 되는 경우 : My hobby is searching the internet.

명사로 쓰일 수 있기 때문에 그냥 to + 동사원형을 쓴다고 해서 목적어로 무조건 오는 것은 아니다. 여기에 그 예를 들어 본다.

I don't know to do

이 문장은 말이 될 것 같다. 해석은 '나는 무엇을 해야 하는지 모른다'.. 그러나 이 문장은 위의 해석을 나타내기 위해서는 부족한 문장이다. 위의 해석대로 문장을 쓰려면 I don't know what to do라고 문장을 써야만 한다.

What to do 무엇을 해야 할지, Where to go 어디로 가야 할지, How to eat 어떻게 먹어야 할지, When to kick 언제 차야 할지, Whether to go 가야 할지 아닌지

그리고 문장의 목적보어로도 쓰일 수 있다는 것도 알 수 있을 것이다.
I force him to do this, 그가 이것을 하도록 내가 강요했다.

형용사적 용법

부정사가 형용사의 역할을 할 수 있다는 것이므로 한정과 서술의 용법으로 쓰일 수 있게 된다.
먼저 한정적 용법으로는 일반적으로 후치(단어의 뒤에서) 수식하게 된다.

I have a lot of paper to write on.
I need a pen to write with.

to write가 paper와 a pen을 수식하고 있는 것이 보일 것이다. 그리고 뒤에 나오는 전치사는 문장의 뜻에 맞게 약간 다르게 오고 있음을 알 수 있다. 이러한 전치사가 오는 것에는 a house to live in, a chair to sit on 등 여러 가지가 있을 수 있을 것이다.

서술적 용법은 말 그대로 동사의 뒤에 나오면서 문장에서 보어가 되는 것을 말하는데 일반적으로 동사의 뒤에 나와서 보어가 되면 문장의 해석에 있어 정해진 의미에 따라 해석해 주어야 하는데 이러한 해석에는 예정, 의무, 가능, 의도, 운명이 있다.

자! 예문을 보자.

We are to go there by three.라는 문장은 우리는 3시까지 가도록 되어 있었다는 말(예정)과 우리는 3시까지 가야 한다(의무), 우리는 3시까지 갈 수 있다(가능), 우리는 3시까지 가야 할 운명이다 라고 해석될 수 있다는 말이다.

그럼 어떨 때 이런 말을 써야 하냐고 묻는다면 그건 여러분이 어떨 때 이 문장을 쓰느냐에 달려있다고 대답하고 싶다.

2형식을 만드는 동사를 잘 알고 있다면 to 부정사의 서술적 용법의 이해가 더욱 쉬울 수 있다.
Seem, come, happen, get, deserve….

부사적 용법

문장을 통해 목적, 원인, 판단, 조건, 결과, 정도를 나타내는데 사용된다. 예문을 읽고 암기하도록 하자.

I go there to see him.

나는 그를 보려고 거기에 갔다. (목적)

I am so happy to see you.

당신을 보니 정말 행복합니다. (원인)

You must be fool to do such a thing.

그런 일을 하는걸 보니 바보임에 틀림없군요. (판단)

I would be happy to get there.

거기에 다다르게 되면 정말 행복할 것 같다. (조건)

He grows up to be a nice man.

그는 자라서 정말 친절한 사람이 되었다. (결과)

It is too heavy to lift.

이것은 너무 무거워서 들 수 없다 (정도)

원형부정사

원형부정사의 용법은 이미 문장의 형식과, 수동태에서 설명했으나 워낙 중요해서 다시 한번 강조하고자 한다.

형태는 to 없이 쓰이는 부정사이고 동사원형만을 쓰는 부정사이다.

먼저 원형부정사는 문장의 동사가 지각동사나 사역동사일 때 그리고 목적어와 목적보어가 능동의 관계에 있으면 반드시 원형부정사가 온다는 것 다시 한번 강조하고 싶다.

You made him do your homework.

부정사의 의미상 주어

문장의 표현에 있어 주어가 너무 길어 It이라는 가주어를 통해 문장을 표현해 주게 될 때 문장의 의미상 주어가 표현되어야 문장이 더 확실히 전달될 수 있는 경우가 있는데 이때 쓰이는 것이 바로 의미상의 주어이다. **(매우 중요!)**

여기에는 문장에 쓰이는 형용사에 따라 의미상의 주어 앞에 쓰이는 전치사가 다른데 반드시 기억해야 한다.

의미상 주어 앞에 for가 오는 경우

It is difficult for you to do this kind of work.

네가 이런 일을 하는 것은 어렵다.

예문에서 it은 to do this kind of work를 받는 말이고 문장의 진짜 주어는 to do this kind of work이고 it은 가주어이다. 그런데 여기서 문장의미상 주어 즉 문장에서 실제로 그 행동의 주체가 되는 것은 you라는 대명사이고 이를 의미상 주어라고 한다.

판단이나 이성적인 상태를 나타내는 형용사가 문장에 나오게 되면 의미상의 주어 앞에는 항상 for가 붙는다.(암기!!) 판단이나 이성적 상태를 나타내는 형용사에는 difficult, natural, possible, strange, hard, necessary, impossible, important 등이 있다.

It is important for him to finish this job by noon,

이 일을 정오까지 끝내는 것은 그에게 있어 중요하다.

의미상 주어 앞에 of가 오는 경우

It is smart of him to finish this job by noon.

그가 이 일을 정오까지 끝내는 것은 현명한 일이다.

예문에서 형용사를 찾아 보면 위의 예문과는 다르게 사람의 성질이나 태도를 나타내고 있는 형용사임을 알 수 있다. 이렇게 사람의 성질이나 태도를 나타내는 형용사(kind, nice, brave, silly, foolish, rude, polite, cruel, careful..)가 나오는 문장은 의미상의 주어 앞에 반드시 전치사 of를 붙여 주어야 한다.

It is rude of her to tell him to do such a thing.

그녀가 그에게 그러한 일을 하라고 말한 것은 예의에 맞지 않는 것이다.

부정사의 시제

부정사도 동사의 성질을 가지고 있어 시제의 표현이 가능한데 여기에는 단순부정사와 완료부정사가 있다.

단순부정사(주절과 종속절의 시제가 일치하거나 한 시제 앞선 경우(Will))

It seems that she is ill = She seems to be ill

I want that I will go there = I want to go there.

완료부정사 to + have + p.p (주절의 동사가 한 시제 뒤쳐진 경우)

It seems that he was ill = He seems to have been ill.

이외에도 희망했던 것들이 이루어지지 못했을 경우에도 사용된다.

He expected to have met her = 그는 그녀를 만날 것을 기대했지만 그러지 못했다.

(중요!!)

동명사

동명사는 명사의 역할을 하게 됨으로 문장에서 주어, 목적어, 전치사의 목적어로 쓰일 수 있다.

Eating too much food is bad for your health.

너무 많이 먹는 것은 건강에 좋지 않다.(주어)

He stops smoking.

그는 담배 피우는 것을 그만 두었다.(목적어)

Seeing is believing

보는 것이 믿는 것이다.(보어)

I am looking forward to seeing you soon.

곧 당신을 만나 뵙기를 기대합니다.(전치사의 목적어)

여기서 매우 중요한 것 한가지 학습해야 할 것 같다. 위의 문장에서 He stop smoking과 같은 경우와 He stop to smoke의 경우, 일반적으로 문장의 뜻이 같을 것으로 생각이 들지만 He stop to smoke는 그는 담배를 피우기 위해 멈춰 섰다로 해석이 되고 He stop smoking의 경우에는 그는 금연했다라고 해석이 된다.

이는 stop의 동사의 경우 동명사만을 목적어로 삼기 때문이다. 목적어를 to 부정사와 동명사로 취해야만 하는 동사는 구분된다는 이야기이다. **매우 중요하다!!**

여기서 먼저 to 부정사와 동명사만을 목적어로 삼는 동사를 각각 나누어 익혀보자.

동명사		To 부정사	
avoid	allow	Agree	Afford
anticipate	Appreciate, admit	Desire	Determine
consider	deny	Decide, Expect	Fail
delay	dislike	Hope	Hesitate
defer	Escape	Mean	Manage, offer
enjoy	Finish	Plan	Pretend
favor	Give up	Promise	Refuse
Help, keep on	Image	Seek	Wish
Mind	Postpone, practice	Want	
Qui, resist	Stop		
Stand	Suggest		

동명사만을 목적어로 삼는다는 말은 동명사가 동사 뒤에 나와야만 문장의 해석이 '– 을, –를' 로 해석된다고 이해하면 된다.

이외에 동명사 to 부정사 모두를 목적어로 취하는 동사가 있다. Prefer, begin, like, hate, continue, start… 일단은 위의 두 가지만 확실히 외워도 지금 거론되는 것은 나중에 좀더 깊이 알 수 있을 것 같다.

이왕 외우기 시작한 거 이것도 완전히 학습해보자. 위의 세 가지 경우를 제외하고 다음과 같은 동사는 동명사를 받을 때 과거사실에 대해서 이야기하고 to 부정사를 받을 때 미래의 사실을 이야기한다는 것을 암기해야 한다.

Regret, remember, forget와 같은 동사는 동명사의 경우 했던 것들을 나타내는데 사용하고 to 부정사는 할 것들에 대해서 이야기할 때 사용된다.

I forget to send him a letter.

그에게 편지 보내야 하는 것을 잊어 버렸다.

I forget sending him a letter.

그에게 편지 보낸 것을 잊어 버렸다.

동명사의 시제

동명사는 명사의 역할을 한다고 들어서 시제는 전혀 관계없을 것 같지만 동사의 성질을 포함하고 있어서 가끔 시제를 표현해 주어야 할 때가 있고 이때 시제의 차이에 따라 단순동명사와 완료동명사를 써주어야 한다.

단순동명사 (주절과 종속질의 시제가 일치하거나 한 시제 앞선 경우(Will))

She is proud that she stands there. = She is proud of standing there.

그녀는 거기에 서 있는 것을 자랑스럽게 여긴다.

She is proud that she will stand there = She is proud of standing there.

그녀는 거기에 서 있게 될 것을 자랑스럽게 생각한다.

완료동명사

I was certain that he had been right.

= I was certain his having been right. 나는 그가 옳았다고 생각했다.

동명사의 의미상 주어

동명사도 부정사와 마찬가지로 의미상의 주어를 가지는 경우가 있는데 여기서는 간단하게만 알아보자.

I don' t like his smoking too much.

나는 그가 너무 많은 담배를 피우는 것을 좋아하지 않는다.

동명사의 관용구

동명사는 관용구의 암기가 중요하다. 다음의 표현과 예문을 암기하도록 해보자.

Be busy –ing : –하느라 바쁘다.

I am busy doing this work. 난 이 일을 하느라 바쁘다.

On –ing : –하자마자.

On leaving to Busan, I was sick. 부산을 떠나자마자 나는 아팠다.

It is no use –ing : –해도 소용없다.

It is no use doing this. 이렇게 하는 것은 아무런 소용이 없다.

Cannot help –ing : –하지 않을 수 없다.

I cannot help leaving her. 나는 그녀를 떠날 수밖에 없었다.

= cannot but + 동사원형

Feel like –ing : –하고 싶은 기분이다.

I feel like doing exercise. 나는 운동을 하고 싶다.

Never –without –ing : –하면 반드시 –한다.

I never sleep without eating something. 나는 잠자기 전에 반드시 무얼 먹는다.

Far from –ing : 결코 –않다.

She is far from doing exercise. 그녀는 결코 운동을 하지 않는다.

A prevent B from –ing : A 때문에 B는 – 하지 못한다.

She prevents him doing something different.

그녀는 B가 다른 것을 하지 못하도록 했다.

Look forward to –ing –을 기대하다.

Object to –ing –을 반대하다.

In addition to –ing –뿐만 아니라.

commit oneself to –ing –에 몰두하다.

분사

To 부정사는 명사, 형용사, 부사적 용법으로 쓰일 수 있고 동명사는 명사로 쓰임으로써 주어, 목적어, 보어의 역할을 할 수 있다는 것을 위의 학습에서 알 수 있었다. 그럼 '분사의 역할을 무엇일까' 라는 의문이 생게게 될 것이다.

'분사는 형용사의 역할을 한다' 는 것을 먼저 알아두자.

그럼 형용사의 학습에서 우리가 알고 있는 형용사의 기능인 수식과 서술의 두 가지 기능을 분사가 할 수 있다는 것을 우리는 또한 알게 될 것이다. 이해가 잘 안 되는 사람은 형용사의 역할에 대한 학습을 다시 하기 바란다.

형용사는 수식과 서술의 역할을 한다.

분사의 형태 : 현재분사 –ing, 과거분사 –ed의 두 가지 형태가 있다. 여기서 동명사의 모양과 분사의 모양이 같고 분사의 모양이 일부 동사의 과거형태와 같다는 것을 또한 알 수 있게 된다. 과거분사는 과거와 과거분사의 형태가 같다는 것은 단어를 외울 때 꽤 봐와서 혼돈이 조금은 적겠지만 동명사와 분사의 구분은 여기서 확실히 해두어야 한다.

다음의 예를 보자.

A living room – a sleeping baby 두 말의 차이에서 같은 –ing 형태의 단어를 쓰지만 분명한 차이가 있는 말을 하고 있다는 거 알 수 있을 것이다.

앞의 예는 응접실(복합명사)이라는 단어를 나타내고 있고 이는 분명 동명사로 쓰이고 있음을 알 수 있다. 그렇지만 뒤의 예는 잠자고 있는 아기라는 말로 잠자고 있다는 형용사가 아기를 수식해 주고 있다는 말로 해석이 되고 이는 sleeping이 형용사의 역할(수식)을 하고 있다는 거 분명히 나타내고 있음을 알 수 있다.

an exciting game (현재분사, 재미있는 게임)

a magnifying glass (동명사, 확대경)

분사의 공부를 조금 더 쉽게 하기 위해서는 다음의 표를 완전히 암기하는 것이 필요하다.

동사의 종류	형태	의미	예문
자동사	현재분사	진행의 의미	Dancing boy 춤을 추고 있는 소년
	과거분사	완료의 의미	Departed grandfather 돌아가신 할아버지
타동사	현재분사	능동의 의미	Exciting game 흥미진진한 게임
	과거분사	수동의 의미	Impressed audience 감명받은 관중

To 부정사에서는 일반적으로 후치수식이(I have nice boy friend to love me) 일반적이지만 분사는 전치와 후치 다 가능하다. 위의 표에서의 예들은 거의 전치의 예를 들고 있어 후치수식의 예를 한가지 들어 본다.

I know the boy laughing at the gate.

문 앞에서 웃고 있는 소년을 알고 있다.

The matter discussed at the conference was not easy topic.

컨퍼런스에서 토론되었던 일은 이해하기 쉬운 주제가 아니다.

여기서 한가지 주의할 점은 'I know the boy laughing at the gate'의 문장에는 'who is'가 생략됐다는 것도 알아야 한다. 이후 관계사 설명하는 부분에서 다시 말하겠지만 이 부분이 생략되면서 분사 단독으로 문장에 남아 그 역할을 하게 된다는 것을 잊지 말자.

I know the boy (who is) laughing at the gate.

이제 분사의 서술적 용법을 이해해 보자. 서술적 용법은 동사의 뒤에 나와서 주어나 목적어의 상태를 설명해주는 형용사를 말하는데 분사는 이 두 가지 역할을 할 수 있다.

She sat laughing at him.

그녀는 앉아서 그 남자를 보고 웃고 있었다.

My grandmother stood surrounded by lots of flower.

할머니는 꽃들에 둘러싸인 채 서있었다.

I saw him running to the finishing line.

나는 그가 결승점에 뛰어 들어오는 것을 보았다.

I heard my name called.

나는 나의 이름이 불려지는 것을 들었다.

위의 용법에 대한 설명과는 조금 다르게 감정을 나타내는 분사는 주어가 사람이냐 사물이냐에 따라 분사의 모양이 바뀌어진다. 여기서 중요한 것은 **사람**일 때는 ed(과거분사)이고 **사물**일 때는 ing(현재진행)을 쓴다는 것 반드시 기억하자.**(매우 중요!!)**

I was board. 나는 지루했다.

He was surprised. 그는 놀랐다.

The speech was boring. 연설을 지루했다.

The game was exciting. 게임은 재미있었다.

분사구문

분사의 학습에 있어 매우 중요한 또한 부분은 분사구문의 이해인데 분사구분은 문장의 반복을 피하고 간단하게 말을 전달하기 위해 종속절의 접속사와 주어를 생략하는 경우를 말한다. 일단 예문을 보자.

When I was there, I could not move any further.

→ Being there, I could not move any further.

위의 문장에서 볼 수 있듯이 주절과 종속절의 주어가 일치하고 동사의 시제가 일치할 때 종속전의 주어와 접속사 생략해주면서 종속절의 동사를 현재분사로 바꾸어주는 것을 분사구분이라고 한다. 물론 현재분사 말고 과거분사가 올 수도 있다.

Because the machine was made by him, it is still in good condition.

→ (Having been) made by him, it is still in good condition.

위의 문장에서는 과거분사가 오는 예를 보여주고 있는데 주절과 종속절의 주어는 일치하지만 시제가 달라 종속절의 문장에서 완료형 분사(having p.p)형태를 가져오게 되고 이 문장에서는 수동태가 쓰여져 있어 having been p.p형태가 와야만 한다. 그리고 수동태나 2형식 문장에서 발생하게 되는 being이나 having been은 생략가능하기 때문에 문장의 맨 앞은 made라는 분사로 시작하게 된다.

자, 아직 조금 이해하기 힘들 수도 있을 것 같아 조금 더 설명해보도록 하겠다.

일단 주절과 종속절의 주어와 시제가 일치하면 무조건 종속절의 주어와 접속사를 생략하고 종속절의 동사를 ing 형으로 바꾸어준다. **(가장 기본적인 원칙, 반드시 기억)**

As she is so nice, she is loved by everyone.

→ Being so nice, she is loved by everyone.

만약 주절과 종속절의 주어는 일치하지만 시제가 주절의 시제보다 종속절의 시제가 앞서는 경우(대과거, 과거)에는 주어를 생략하고 having p.p형태로 바꾸어준다. (두 번째 원칙)

As she was so beautiful, she is still loved by everyone.

→ Having been so beautiful, she is still loved by everyone.

문장의 맨 앞에 being이나 having been이 오게 되면 이 두 가지는 생략이 가능하게 된다. 그러니까 위의 문장에서 Being so nice, she is loved by everyone. 경우 앞에 있는 being을 생략하고 so nice, she is loved by everyone.이라고 쓰게 된다. 그리고 Because the machine was made by him, it is still in good condition. → (Having been) made by him, it is still in good condition. 문장에서 역시 having been이라는 단어들이 앞에 나와서 이것들을 생략하고 문장을 쓸 수 있게 된다.

과제

To 부정사의 3가지 용법을 이용하여 3문장을 만들어 보고 동명사와 분사의 차이를 설명해 봅시다.

동명사와 to 부정사를 목적어로 받는 동사를 노트에 다시 한번 정리합니다.

단어장 정리

실전 문제

※ 다음 문장에서 틀린 부분을 찾아 바르게 고쳐 쓰시오.

1. Our team enjoyed to do those tasks at that time.

2. You need to stop to smoke for your health.

3. We are looking forward to meet you next time.

4. They made this work to do by us.

5. Our security team decided adapting new system for better working environment.

※ 다음 내용에서 적절한 단어를 찾아내시오.

6. The lecture (taught/ teaching) by new lecturer need to be reviewed.

7. The hotel was full of the audience (taking/ taken) pictures.

8. We decided to hire (retired/ retire) workers for marketing purpose.

※ 빈칸에 알맞은 말을 고르시오.

9. The new department will have a key role in __________ new standard for next few years.

a) Setting up b) Set up
c) have set up d) to set up

10. It is very nice ________ to tell them your appreciation.

a) of you b) for you
c) you d) to you

11. If you consider current your situation, you _________leave this place is not strange.

a) may well b) cannot help
c) may as well d) nothing but

12. We have been here since this morning, but we never felt __________.

a) boring b) bored
c) to bore d) bore

13. The board ____________ to hold the conference in Hamilton hotel, we were surprised.

a) decided b) deciding
c) to decide d) decision

09 접속사 & 관계사

접속사와 관계사는 일반적으로 나누어서 공부해야 하지만 여기서 한꺼번에 공부하는 것은 이 두 가지가 시험에 같이 출제되고 쓰임에 있어서도 두 가지의 다른 용법이 구분이 힘들게 느껴질 때가 많기 때문이다. 하지만 두 가지는 문장의 연결이라는 공통성을 가지고 있다는 것 반드시 기억하자. 자 먼저 아래 그림을 보자.

접속사	두 문장의 형태가 그대로 남아 있다. (접속사 뒤에 완전한 문장이 온다)	I want to go there, because I like to see what happen in there.
관계사	관계사 뒤에 오는 문장은 문장의 한 요소가 빠져 있다. (관계사 뒤에 나오는 문장은 불완전한 문장이 온다)	I like him who is my boy friend.

또 한가지 기억해야 할 것은 하나의 문장에는 하나의 동사가 온다는 것이고 두 개의 동사가 문장에 오려면 반드시 접속사나 관계사가 있어야 한다.

먼저 접속사를 알아 보자.

접속사의 종류 : 등위접속사, 상관접속사, 종속 접속사

등위 접속사 : and, but, or, nor, for

등위 접속사의 가장 기본적인 원칙은 등위 접속사의 앞뒤에는 같은 형태의 품사끼리 연결한다는 것 기억하자. 즉 앞에 명사가 오면 뒤에 명사가 와야 하고 앞에 형용사가 오면 뒤에 형용사가 와야 하고 앞에 to 부정사가 오면 뒤에도 to 부정사가 와야 한다는 것이다.

And

You and I are interested in same subject.

너와 나는 같은 과목에 관심을 가지고 있다.

She sings and dances at the same time.

그녀는 노래하고 춤도 추었다.

Move faster and you get more.

빨리 움직이면 더 많은 것을 얻게 된다.

She is nice and beautiful.

그녀는 친절하고 아름답다.

명사 and 명사로 연결된 명사가 문장의 앞에 와서 주어가 되면 복수 취급해야 하는 것이 원칙이지만 일부 명사의 경우 항상 같이 와서 쓰이는 경우에는 단수 취급하는 경우도 있다.

Whisky and soda is my favorite mix. 위스키소다는 내가 좋아하는 음료이다.

Trial and error is good teacher for our life. 시행착오는 인생에 좋은 스승이다.

But

We all like him, but she didn't like him.

우리 모두는 그를 좋아했지만 그녀는 그를 좋아하지 않았다.

He is not a student, but a teacher.

그는 학생이 아니라 선생이다.

Or

She or I have to this. 그녀 아니면 내가 이것을 해야 한다.

(or 뒤에 나오는 명사를 중심으로 동사를 선택하고 사용한다)

Hurry up, or you will be late. 서두르지 않으면 늦게 된다.

Nor

You cannot finish this now, nor can you quit right now.

너는 지금 이것을 끝낼 수도 없고 그만둘 수도 없다.

(도치된다는 것 명심하자)

For

You have to go there, for someone is expecting you.

너는 반드시 거기에 가야 한다. 왜냐하면 어떠한 사람이 너를 보려고 기다리고 있다.

상관접속사(Either A or B, Neither A nor B, Both A and B, Not only A but also B, A as well as B)

상관접속사는 등위접속사에서 배운 것을 활용하는 것이라고 생각하면 된다. 그래서 여러 가지 등위접속사가 같이 쓰이고 있는 것을 볼 수 있을 것이다. 상관접속사는 먼저 어떠한 상관접속사가 있는지 암기하고 난 후 각 접속사의 덩어리가 주어로 올 때와 목적어로 올 때 그 쓰임에 대해 기억해두면 된다. 뭘 말하는 건지..이해가 잘 안 된다고!!

자, 밑에 제시되는 예문과 설명을 보자.

Either A or B, Neither A nor B는 주어로 쓰일 때가 있고 목적어로 쓰일 때가 있다.

주어로 쓰일 때 Either he or I have to this.

이 문장에서 동사인 have to의 주어는 he가 아니라 I이다. 만약 he가 주어였다면 뒤에 나오는 동사는 has가 되었어야 할 것이다.

다음은 목적어로 쓰일 때이다. She will choose either him or me.

앞에 문장에서 either과 or 사이에 나왔던 인칭은 분명 주격 (He, I)이었지만 목적어로 쓰인 경우에는 목적격(him, me)이 들어간 것을 볼 수 있을 것이다. 어찌보면 너무나 당연한 것처럼 보이겠지만 많은 학생들이 이 부분이 문제로 출제되면 대책이 없는 것처럼 보여서 여기에서 강조하고자 한다.

Either A or B, Neither A nor B가 주어로 쓰일 때는 동사와 가까운 것이 주어이고 목적어로 쓰이게 되면 상관접속사의 사이에는 목적격을 써주어야 한다.

Both A and B도 주어로 쓰일 때와 목적어로 쓰일 때가 있다.

주어로 쓰일 때 Both You and I are going to go there. 너와 내가 거기에 갈 예정이다. 여기서 are라는 동사는 앞에 you가 주어가 되었기 때문에 온 것이 아니라 주어가 복수 주어이기 때문에 are가 온 것이다. 다시 말하자면 Both I and you를 받는 동사는 위의 예와 같이 are가 와야 한다는 것이다. Both I and you are going to go there. 나와 당신이 거기에 갈 예정이다. 물론 동사가 be 동사로 안 쓰이는 경우에는 복수주어의 동사를 써주면 된다.

Both you and I have to work together.

당신과 나는 같이 일해야만 한다.

목적어로 쓰이는 경우 I like both her and him. 위에서 말한 것처럼 목적어로 쓰일 경우 상관접속사 사이에 쓰이는 인칭대명사는 목적격이 와야 한다.

Both A and B가 주어로 쓰이게 되면 반드시 복수 주어의 동사를 취하게 되고 목적어로 쓰이게 되면 A, B는 목적격을 써주어야 한다.

Not only A but also B, B as well as A도 주어로 쓰일 때와 목적어로 쓰일 때가 있다. 그리고 둘 다 같은 의미를 나타낸다고 할 수 있다. 뜻은 'A뿐만 아니라 B도' 라는 뜻이다.

주어로 쓰일 때 Not only he but also you are happy with her. 그 뿐만 아니라 너도 그녀와 함께 행복했다. (문장의 동사인 are는 you가 주어로 쓰이기 때문이다. 그리고 상관접속사 사이의 인칭대명사의 격은 주격으로 쓰인 것, 다시 한번 살펴보자) 위의 문장과 같은 문장은 You as well as He are happy with her이고 여기서는 문장의 동사는 앞에 나오는 you임을 보고 익혀야 할 것이다. (Not only A but also B = B as well as A)

목적어로 쓰이는 경우는

I like not only him but also her.

나는 그뿐만 아니라 그녀도 좋아한다.

(목적격으로 쓰이고 있는 것 역시 다시 한번 확인하자)

종속 접속사(that, if, whether, because, when, while, as, since, as soon as, though, so –that, so that)

종속접속사는 시험에 나와서 공부한다는 것보다는 문장의 이해를 위해 필수적이다. 따라서 문장을 통해 익히고 쓸 수 있어야 한다. 그리고 종속절의 역할들(명사, 부사)에 대한 이해가 필수적이다.

명사적 역할을 하는 접속사	형용사적 역할을 하는 관계대명사	부사적 역할을 하는 접속사
That : I knew that he is crazy. 나는 그가 미쳤다는 거 알고 있었어. (목적어) Our problem is that we are not concern each other. 우리의 문제는 서로를 걱정하지 않는다는 거야. (보어) It was nice that you gave her a present. 당신이 그녀에게 선물을 준 것은 정말 잘 한 일이에요! (주어)	I call him who can help me. 나를 도와줄 그를 불렀다. 여기서 주의할 것은 여기서 who는 관계대명사이다. 이 부분은 관계사 설명하는 부분에서 자세히 다룰 것이다.	Because : I like him because he always shows me some respect. 그는 항상 날 이해해 줄려고 노력하기 때문에 난 그를 좋아해. When: When I was there, I could not see anything. 내가 거기에 갔을 때 난 아무것도 볼 수 없었어. While I was eating a meal, I saw her. 내가 밥을 먹고 있을 때 난 그녀를 보았어.
If : I want to know if (whether) you love me or not. 난 당신이 나를 좋아하는지 안 하는지 알고 싶어.		As: As he walked in, she was leaving. 그가 걸어 들어올 때 그녀는 떠나고 있었다.
I don't know what you want to do. 난 당신이 무얼 하기를 원하는지 모르겠어. 여기서 what you want to do는 간접의문문이라고 하는 것이다. (의문사+주어+동사)		Since : We have eaten anything since we arrived there. 우리가 거기에 간 이후로 우리는 아무것도 먹지 못했다. since는 because가 될 수도 있음 As soon as : We all noticed that as soon as we got in. 우리가 거기에 들어가자마자 우리는 그것을 알아 차렸다.
		Though : I did my best though I was really sick. 아팠음에도 불구하고 나는 최선을 다했었다. So -that : It was so bright that I could see everything. 거기는 너무 밝아서 거기에 있는 모든 것을 볼수 있었다. So that : I ran again so that nobody could see me properly. 아무도 볼 수 없도록 나는 다시 뛰기 시작했다.

간접의문문은 그 순서가 학습의 핵심이다. 즉 원래 의문문은 의문사 + 조동사 주어 + 동사 순인데 이러한 문장이 다른 문장의 한 부분으로 들어가게 되면 의문사 + 주어 + 동사의 순이 된다는 것이다. 다음의 문장들을 보면서 그 순서에 대해서 익혀보자.

You are a student → Are you a student? → Why are you a student?
→ I don't know why you are a student.

관계사

관계사는 다음의 표를 일단 먼저 자세히 보자. 물론 나중에 이 표를 완전히 암기해야 한다.

선행사	주격	목적격	소유격
사람	Who	Whom (who)	Whose
사람, 동물	Which	Which	Whose (of which)
사람 / 사물, 동물 선행사가 의문사인 경우, 최상급, 서수	That	That	
선행사 포함	what	what	
사람의 지위, 성격, 지위, 신분	Which She is nice girl which you are. 그녀는 너같이 친절한 여자이다.		
선행사가 구, 절 그리고 형용사인 경우 which 앞에, 가 오고 문장을 만듦	Which She is nice, which you are not 그녀는 친절하지만 너는 아니다.		

주격 관계 대명사

I have a friend who is from Australia.

나는 호주에서 온 친구가 있다.

위의 문장은 주격 관계대명사를 써서 문장을 이어주는 예이다. 쉽게 말하면 뒤에 나오는 문장에서 주어가 생략되어 있다는 말이기도 하다. 이 문장은 I have a friend + He is from Australia. 의 두 개의 문장이 결합되어 쓰여진 것이다. 이 두 문장의 사이에 who라는 주격 관계 대명사가 와서 뒤의 문장의 he를 대신하여 문장의 주어 역할을 하면서 문장을 연결하게 된다. 여기서 a friend는 선행사라고 하는 것이고 선행사가 사람이므로 주격 관계대명사인 who를 써 준 것이다.

I have a map which can help us to find a way.

우리에게 길을 알려줄 수 있는 지도를 나는 가지고 있다.

(주격관계대명사(which), 선행사=사물)

I know him and his dog that used to live in my town.

나는 나의 동네에 옛날에 살았던 그와 그의 개를 안다.

(주격관계대명사(that), 선행사=사람+사물)

that은 사람과 사물을 다 선행사로 받을 수 있고 선행사가 최상급이나 서수, 의문사가 올 때에도 사용될 수 있다. 여기서 주의할 것은 That 앞에는 절대 ,(쉼표)가 오지 않고 전치사도 오지 않는다는 것 반드시 기억해두자.

Who that has conscience would do such a thing?

양심이 있는 사람이면 누가 그런 짓을 할 수 있겠는가?

He is the best student that has so much knowledge in this field.

그는 이 분야에서 많은 지식을 알고 있는 가장 우수한 학생이다.

관계대명사는 시험에서 매우 비중이 높다. 하지만 관계대명사의 출제 유형은 다른 문법과는 다르게 유형에 정형화 되어 있어서 위에 제시한 표를 완전히 암기하고 문장의 수의 일치 관계만 확실히 파악한다면 전혀 문제될 게 없는 부분이기도 하다. 즉 적절한 관계대명사를 찾아내고 관계대명사와 그 뒤에 나오는 동사와의 관계를 이해하면 된다는 것이다.

자! 그럼 목적격 관계 대명사로 들어가기 전에 관계대명사의 수의 일치 부분 한번 정리해보자.

단수	I like him who is my brother.	관계대명사의 뒤에 나오는 동사는 선행사의 수와 일치시킨다. 여기서는 him은 단수이라서 단수동사 is가 쓰임
복수	I like them who are my friends.	여기서 선행사는 them이고 선행사가 복수라서 동사는 복수동사인 are를 써줌

시험을 위한 팁

관계 대명사에서 자주 출제되는 문제는 삽입절이 들어있는 문장이다. 다음의 예를 보자 You met them who I have known them for many years were my previous teachers. 자! 여기서 선행사는 them이고 관계대명사는 who이고 그 관계대명사를 이어주는 동사는 were이다. 문제는 많은 학생들이 이 문장이 목적격 관계대명사를 취하는 문장인 줄 착각하여 who 대신에 whom이 와야 하는 걸로 착각하는 경우가 많고 단순히 뒤에 나오는 문장의 구조를 보고 접속사를 넣어야 하는 문장으로 착각하는 경우가 많다는 것이다. 그리고 뒤에 나오는 동사도 were가 와야 한다는 사실을 잘 모른다는 것이다. I have known them for many years는 삽입절로 문장의 수식절일 뿐이고 관계대명사의 역할에는 아무런 관계가 없다는 걸 알아야 한다.

목적격 관계대명사

말 그대로 관계대명사가 문장에서 목적어의 역할을 한다는 것이다.

I watched the movie which they have already seen.

그들이 이미 보았던 영화를 나는 보았다.

예문에서 보여지는 것과 같이 which가 받는 것은 영화이고 이 명사는 뒤의 문장에서 목적어를 지칭하는 것이고 문장에서 빠져있다.

The lady who (whom) I met today is my aunt.

내가 오늘 만났던 여자는 나의 아줌마이다.

(목적격관계대명사 Who, whom, 선행사=사람)

The gift which we gave him was very expensive.

우리가 그에게 주었던 선물은 매우 비싼 것이었다.

(목적격 관계 대명사 which, 선행사=사물)

목적격 관계 대명사의 특징은 문장에서 생략될 수 있다는 것이다.

소유격 관계대명사

I like this picture whose colors are unbelievable.

나는 그림의 색깔이 너무 아름다운 이 그림을 좋아한다.

I like this picture. + The colors of this picture are unbelievable.

위의 문장은 다른 두 가지로 표현이 가능한데

그 한가지는 I like this picture of which the colors are unbelievable.이고 다른 한가지는 I like this picture the colors of which are unbelievable.

What

What은 관계대명사로 쓸 경우 주의할 것은 what이 선행사를 포함한다는 것이다. 그래서 what 앞에는 선행사가 없다.

That is not what is for this process.

그것은 이 작업을 위해 있는 것이 아니다. (주격)

She is not what you know.

그녀는 당신이 알고 있는 여자가 아니다. (목적격)

복합 관계대명사

종류 : Whoever 누구나, Whomever 누구에게나, Whatever 무엇이나, Whichever 어느 것이나

특징 : 선행사가 없다.

Someone whoever comes first will be served.

누구든 가장 먼저 오는 사람이 서비스를 받을 것이다.

I will promise to give my best service whomever you send me.

당신이 보내는 어떤 사람도 나는 최선을 다해 서비스할 것을 약속한다.

관계부사

관계부사는 관계대명사와는 다르게 뒤에 완전한 문장이 온다. 그 이유는 관계부사는 시간, 장소, 방법, 이유를 나타내는 문장을 표현하기 때문이다.

I know the time when we have to leave.

나는 우리가 언제 떠나야 하는지 알고 있다.

This is the place where we serve our conference.

우리가 컨퍼런스를 하는 장소는 바로 여기이다.

Tell me the reason why she doesn' t like this dish.

왜 그녀가 이 음식을 좋아하지 않는지 알려주세요.

This is the way how we cook food.

이게 바로 우리가 요리를 하는 방법이다.

과제

관계사와 접속사의 다른 점은 무엇인지 예문을 통해 설명해 보세요.

상관접속사 2가지를 들고 예문을 만들어 봅시다.

관계대명사 표를 다시 한번 정리하고 설명해 봅시다.

관계부사와 복합 관계대명사의 종류를 들고 문장 하나씩 만들어 봅시다.

단어장 정리

실전 문제

※ 다음 빈칸에 알맞은 말을 넣으시오.

1. I thought he was ___ a doctor, but a nurse.

2. ______ you and I thought the same way.

3. Either you and I ___ in the wrong.

4. ________ they will visit here or not is clear.

※ 다음 빈칸에 알맞은 말을 고르시오.

5. It is up to you _________ you will take it or not.

a) whether b) that
c) nor d) what

6. You as well as I _____ will pass this exam.

a) is b) are
c) to be d) being

7. Currently, there are more than 12 nations________ the organization.

a) that they compose b) that compose
c) compose d) they compose it

8. Jim is the man ______ is known to the best athlete in our school.

a) who　　b) whom
c) whose　　d) of which

9. A : Do you know anyone to carry those?

B : I know the man ______ could this job properly.

a) is　　b) which
c) who　　d) whoever

10. A : Who do you thinks should get this prize?

B : You can give the prize to ________ you think did the most.

a) whomever　　b) whoever
c) anyone　　d) whichever

※ 문장의 틀린 곳을 찾아 고치시오.

11. Rice is our main source of our meal, so sometimes we need to eat bread instead.

12. Either the cold weather, it is necessary to do some extra work for protection.

13. There are not many people in this town which own the building.

14. The meeting had only 30guests, all of whom was the friend of mine.

15. The manager and supervisor could not agree about whose should be done to this matter.

16. Everyone did not know the location which the new building was built.

17. She got engaged in October where is in her favorite season.

18. A chemical compound that cause a serious harm to people should be banned.

10 가정법

많은 학생들이 가정법을 힘들다고 하는 것을 들었다. 그런데 실제로 가정법처럼 문법의 개념 학습만으로 그 전체적인 내용을 단번에 알 수 있는 문법도 드물다. 하지만 학생들이 어렵다고 느끼는 데는 실전문제에서 조금은 어렵게 문제가 출제되고 단어의 수준이 너무 높아 그러할 것이라는 것이 저자의 생각이다. 따라서 가정법의 극복을 위해서는 기본개념을 확실히 외우고 단어 학습에 좀더 박차를 가한다면 분명 효과를 볼 것이라 생각한다.

가정법의 의미 : 가정법은 상황의 가정, 소망, 후회, 회상, 과거의 행동이 현재의 미친 영향 그리고 일어나기 힘들 수 있는 상황 등을 표현하고자 할 때 사용된다.

먼저 가정법의 공부를 위해 다음의 표를 완전히 머릿속에 넣어 두자.

용법	문장 시제	의미	예문	기타
현재	현재 + 미래 현재 + 현재	일어날 가능성이 많은 일들을 표현하고자 할 때, 시제 배울 때 시간소건부사절이라고도 배웠다.	If it rains tomorrow, We won't go camping. 내일 비가 오면 우리는 캠핑을 가지 않을 것이다.	주장, 제안, 요구, 명령, 필요, 당연 등의 미래표현에 있어 that절 이하에 should+원형이 온다는 원칙 기억하자
과거	과거 + 과거 (would)	현재 사실과는 반대의 것들을 소망할 때, 일어날 가능성 거의 없음(그러나 불가능은 없다는 거 잊지 맙시다)	If I had money, I would buy this hotel. 내가 돈이 있다면 이 호텔을 살 텐데..	가정법과거의 다른 세가지 표현 I wish I would have enough money. 내가 돈이 있었다면.. It is right (high, about) time we work harder. 이제 우리가 더욱 열심히 일해야 할 때이다. If I were you, I wouldn't do that. 내가 너라면 그렇게 하시 않을 거야.

과거완료	과거완료 + would have p.p	과거의 사실에 대한 후회, 회상을 표현할 때	If you had arrived there just ten minutes earlier, you could have left there with them. 10분만 일찍 도착했어도 그 사람들과 같이 출발할 수 있었을 텐데.	I wish I had been there. 거기에 있었음 좋았을 텐데 (거기에 가지 못했다)
혼합	과거완료 + 과거 (would)	과거의 사실이 현재의 상태에 영향을 미치고 있음을 표현할 때	If you had not helped me, I would not be here now. 당신이 와주지 않았더라면 난 여기 없었을 거야.	
미래	Should + 조동사 + 동사원형	자신의 기준으로 보아 가능성이 없다고 생각될 때 (그렇게 되지 않겠지만 만약 -하다면 이럴 것이다)	If you should experience any malfunctions of this product, please contact our service department. 만약 제품에 문제가 발견된다면 저희 서비스팀으로 연락 부탁 드립니다.	If any visitors should come. I won't say anything. 만약 누가 온다면 아무것도 말하지 않을게요.

위에서 보여지듯이 가정법은 현재를 나타내기 위해 과거를 쓰고 과거를 나타내기 위해 과거완료를 써서 표현하고 있음을 인식하자.

위의 설명에서 가정법 현재 부분의 기타부분에서 제시되었던 설명에 대한 추가적인 설명하고자 한다.

문장의 동사가 주장(insist), 제안(suggest, propose), 충고(advise, recommend), 요구(demand,. Request), 명령(order)이나 가주어와 동사 다음에 나오는 형용사가 중요(important), 필요나 필수적(essential, necessary) 인 것을 나타내고 미래지향적인 이야기를 표현하고자 할 때 문장 아래에 나오는 that 절 이하의 표현에는 반드시 should + 원형의 시제를 써주게 되고 should 를 생략하게 된다.

말이 좀 어렵네.. 예문을 보자.

She insisted that we (should) work harder.

그녀는 우리가 더욱 열심히 일해야 한다고 주장했다.

이 문장에서 should가 보통 생략된다고 했기 때문에 she insisted that we work harder.라고 표현해야 하고 이러한 표현은 문법적으로 맞지 않는 것처럼 보이지만 위에서 말해진 조건들 즉 문장의 동사가 주장을 나타내고 과거기는 하지만 그 당시의 미래에 대한 이야기이므로 문법적으로 맞는 말이 된다.

한가지 주의할 점은 만약 문장의 의미가 미래지향이 아닌 단순한 사실을 말할 때는 주절의 시제와 목적절의 시제를 일치시켜 주어야 한다는 것이다.

She insisted that she was there.

그녀는 자기가 거기에 있었다고 주장했다. (단순한 사실)

As if + 과거(마치 -인 것처럼), 과거완료(마치 -였던 것처럼)

He talks as if she were there.

그는 그녀가 거기에 있는 것처럼 말한다.

He talks as if she had been there.

그는 그녀가 거기에 있었던 것처럼 말한다.

Unless = If not

You will fail your exams unless you work harder.

더 열심히 공부하지 않는다면 시험에 합격할 수 없게 된다.

가정법의 다른 표현들

I will come only if nothing is said to the press.

언론에 아무것도 말하지 않겠다고 보장하면 거기에 갈 것이다.

If only he had a car.

그가 차가 있었으면 좋겠다.

If 의 생략

가정법에서 if가 생략되어서 문장이 표현되는 경우가 많은데 이럴 때는 조건절의 주어와 동사가 도치되어서 나타난다. 반드시 기억하자. 공식적인 언어 표현에서 많이 사용되기도 한다. 일반적으로 조건절에 had, should, were 등의 동사가 나오고 if를 생략하면서 문장의 주어와 동사의 위치를 바꾸어주게 된다.

Should people decide to hold a meeting, we would welcome it.
= If people should decide to hold a meeting, we would welcome it.
사람들이 회의를 하겠다고 결정하게 된다면 우리는 그 사실을 환영하게 될 것이다.

Had I known, I would not have done it.
= If I had known, I would not have done it.
만약 내가 알았더라면 그것을 하지 않았을 것이다.

과제

가정법의 다른 5가지 형태에 따른 여러분만의 예문을 만들어 봅시다.

가정법의 표에서 기타에 해당되는 부분을 기억하는지요? 무슨 내용이 있었는지 설명해 봅시다.

단어장 정리

실전 문제

※ 괄호 안의 알맞은 단어를 골라 문장을 완성하여 다시 쓰시오.

1. We will stay home if it (will rain, rains) tomorrow.

____

2. She will give you a ride if she (will drive, drives) tomorrow.

____

3. Unless she comes home before dinner, we (will order, order) pizza.

____

4. If you (don't, won't) do your homework now, you can't finish it on time.

____

5. If you park your car here, the police (will givc, gives) you a ticket.

____

괄호 안의 주어진 단어를 적절히 고쳐 빈칸을 채워 문장을 다시 쓰시오.

6. If you _______ (leave, not) early, you will miss the train.

____

7. If it _______ (snow), we will make snowman outside.

____

8. Unless I _______ (be, not) busy tomorrow, I will visit my grandparents.

____

9. You should tell your teacher unless you _______ (come) to class tomorrow.

____

10. She tends to forget things if she _______ (take, not) notes.

____

※ 다음 문장을 읽고 어색한 부분을 바르게 고쳐 문장을 다시 쓰시오.

11. I give you my old computer if I buy a new one.

____

12. I wonder if he invites me to his party.

____

13. If you will see Tony, please tell him hello for me.

____

14. You be hungry if you don't eat now.

____

15. If you will ask me, I will be glad to help you anytime.

____

16. I'd like to know if it snows tomorrow or not.

____

※ 주어진 한글 뜻에 맞게 문장을 영어로 쓰시오.

17. 서두르지 않으면 당신을 마지막 기차를 놓칠 것입니다. (if, hurry, the last train)

____

18. 그녀는 지금 집에 가도 되는지 알고 싶어합니다. (want)

____

19. 만일 그것이 사실이라면, 그 남자는 무죄일 것입니다. (not guilty)

____

※ 다음 문장에서 어색한 부분을 찾아 고쳐 쓰시오.

20. If I <u>have learned</u> this system <u>properly</u>, it would be <u>much easier</u> for me <u>to do</u> this job.

21. Had she finished this job a little bit sooner, she would had gone to there.

22. She insisted that he works harder for the next project.

23. Was I rich, I could go to Singapore.

24. It is time you go there.

11 전치사

모든 문법공부가 그러하겠지만 전치사의 공부는 절대 개념정리만 하고 끝내서는 안 된다. 수없이 많은 표현들이 전치사와 같이 쓰이면서 공부해야 하고(수동태의 관용구를 참조) 이러한 표현들을 통해서 한 단계 발전된 표현과 정확한 언어의 쓰임을 이해할 수 있게 된다.

시간의 전치사

At	시점	At noon, at 10 o' clock, at that time	At Christmas 크리스마스에
On	요일, 날짜	On Friday, on new year's day, on 21th of December	On the weekend 주말에
In	계절, 연, 월	In May, in 2000, in winter	In a minute. 일분간

By(-까지, 행위의 완료) / till(-까지, 행위의 계속)

She has to finish this work by 8 o' clock.

그녀는 이 일을 8시까지 끝내야 한다.

We will stay here till tomorrow.

우리는 여기에 내일까지 있게 될 것이다.

For (구체적인 기간) / during(특정기간)

We had lived in Adelaide for two years.

우리는 2년 동안 에들레이드에 있었다.

We had lived in Adelaide during two years. 이러한 표현은 쓸 수 없다.

We had lived in Adelaide during those two years.

우리는 그 2년 동안 에들레이드에 있었다.

장소 및 방향의 전치사

On	위에, 바로 위 / beneath (바로 아래)	The pen is on the desk
Over	위에 일반적으로 수직적인 위를 말할 때 / under (아래)	look over there. 위의 저기를 보아라
In	안에	I put the pen in the box. 상자 안에 넣어놨어
Above	위에, 비스듬한 위, 일정한 기준으로부터 위에 / below 아래에	Everything became red below the bridge. 다리 아래의 모든 것이 빨갛게 변했다.
Between	사이에(둘 사이), among(셋 이상), beside(곁에), next to(두 지점 사이에서 서로를 지칭할 때)	I was standing between two tree.
To	-으로. Toward(-쪽으로, 향하여), for (방향, 도착지, -을 향해서)	She went to the office. 그녀는 사무실로 갔다. She went toward the building. 그녀는 빌딩을 향해 갔다. Next train is for Busan. 다음기차는 부산행이다.
At	지점, in(도시, 국가, 비교적 넓은 지역)	At home, at school. In Daegu.
Up	위로 올라가는, down 아래로 내려가는	The man was climbing up the mountain. 남자는 산을 올라가고 있었다.
Across	가로질러(횡단), through(통과하여), along(따라서)	I across the street. 거기를 가로질러 갔다.
In front of	-의 앞에, in rare of(뒤에), back(바로 뒤에)	I was standing in front of the building. 나는 그 빌딩의 앞에 서 있었다.

원인 / 이유의 전치사

For, with, from, of －때문에

I felt bad for his behavior.

그의 행동이 나를 불쾌하게 했다.

I could do anything with excitement.

흥분해서 아무것도 할 수 없었다.

I was tired from too much homework.

너무 많은 숙제로 피로했다.

She died of cancer.

그녀는 암으로 죽었다.

(of는 좀더 구체적인 것들 보통 쓰게 된다)

Because/ because of －때문에

이유나 원인을 나타내는 대표적인 전치사와 전치사구이지만 그 쓰임이 달라 시험에도 자주 나오고 표현에 있어서도 주의를 요한다. Because는 뒤에 절이 나오고 because of는 뒤에 명사나 구가 나온다.

I was so happy because she was there.

그녀가 거기에 있어서 매우 행복했나.

I was happy because of her.

그녀 때문에 나는 행복했다.

목적, 수단, 재료, 양보

I will do everything for achieving my dream.

나는 나의 꿈을 이루기 위해 모든 것을 다할 것이다.

You have to cut those with knife.

그것들은 칼을 가지고 잘라야 한다.

This desk is made of log.

이 책상은 통나무로 만들어졌다.

Butter is made from milk.

169버터는 우유로 만들어진다.

Flour is made into that snack.

밀가루로 이러한 과자를 만든다.

Despite (In spite of) her mistake, she did a good job.

실수에도 불구하고 그녀는 일을 잘해내었다.

Although she was not very happy, she did her best.

그녀는 행복하지 않았음에도 불구하고 일을 잘해 내었다.

(위의 문장과 비교할 때 의미는 비슷하지만 although는 뒤에 절이 와있음을 눈 여겨 보자.)

과제

장소에 관계된 전치사를 그림을 이용하여 한번 표현해 봅시다.

시간과 관련된 전치사를 이용하여 문장 10개를 만들어 봅시다.

단어장 정리

실전 문제

※ 다음 빈칸에 들어갈 적절한 전치사를 쓰시오.

1. There is something wrong ____ this machine.

2. They have lived here ______ 1999.

3. I have lived here _______ 12 years.

4. She will be back here ______ 11 o'clock.

5. I am familiar ______ this product.

6. The airplane was flying _______ our head.

※ 다음 문장에서 틀린 부분을 골라 내시오,

7. They provide the poor to food.

8. Ladies and gentlemen, we are going to leave from Sydney. Please fasten your seat belts.

9. The hotel are looking for the people to do this job by supervisor in the restaurant.

10. When I told you by the telephone, we will buy the products on better conditions.

Part Ⅲ

Interview, Resume, CV Letter

01 인터뷰 영어

영어로 인터뷰하는 과정은 한국어로 하는 인터뷰과정과 크게 차이가 없다. 하지만 질문과 대답에 있어 영어적인 표현방식에 익숙한 사람이 표현하는 말과 한국말을 그대로 번역해서 말하는 사람에게는 많은 차이가 있을 수 있다. 여기서 한가지 강조하고자 하는 것은 영어적인 표현은 한번에 익혀지는 것은 아니지만 반복해서 연습하고 말하려고 노력한다면 될 수 있다는 것 강조하고 싶다.

인터뷰에서 가장 많이 묻는 질문의 유형은 다음과 같다.

1. 본인에 관한 것
2. 지원한 일과 회사에 관한 것
3. 자신의 교육과 경험에 관한 것들을 묻는 질문이 있을 수 있을 것이다.

자! 이제 여기서 나오는 내용들을 보면서 질문 하나하나에 자신의 입장을 생각하면서 정리해보자.

Frequently asked job interview questions(많이 묻는 질문들)

Question about yourself(본인에 관한 것)

Would you introduce yourself?
Could you tell us about yourself?

가장 흔한 질문이지만 가장 어려운 질문 중에 하나이다. 반드시 준비해 가야 하는 질문이기도 하다. 긍정적이고 밝은 생각을 남겨줄 수 있는 말을 해야 할 것이고 반드시 내가 이 조직에 도움이 될 수 있을 것이라는 말을 잊지 말아야 한다.

성격의 묘사를 통한 자기소개

예1) It is not easy to say who I am exactly. But I am a sort of person who can be easily friend and I think I always try to be a better friend too. I am also good at talking with someone. I love to talk with anyone. Someone may say I am bit too talkative but I love who I am.

예2) I am bit quiet and bit of shy, but lots of friends told me that I am a good listener. I love to listen to what others say. I think we need those skills as a person who works in hospitality industry.

I started my college education bit later than others. But I think I did lots more than any others and I have learnt so much so far. I always have positive mind to do any work and I am good at listen to others' story. I think those will help me to be a better service person. I want to have this chance sincerely and I am ready to do it.

Could you tell us about your family or hometown?

가족 한 사람 한 사람에 대한 소개도 중요하지만 가족이나 여러분의 주위의 사람들을 통해 무엇을 배웠느냐가 가장 중요한 일이고 이것들을 말해줄 수 있어야 한다.

예1) When I mention on my family I always say about my father. Kind gentleman with so much energy, all I can do now are all from him. But I have to say he is also just one person as a human being. I learn also from that fact too.

예2) I love to talk about my family. I cannot say my family is ideal but when I consider myself as a good friend, good neighbor, and good student. I think I learn all things for becoming those from my family. I still have to say sometimes I have argument with my brother… I love my family sincerely.

What is your greatest strength or weakness?
Please describe your personality?
What do your friends tell you about yourself?
Do you have any hobbies, outside interests, participate in any sports?

위의 질문은 여러분의 성격, 장점과 단점에 대한 질문이다. 여러분이 기술한 이력서와 자기소개서 외에도 인터뷰 당일에 자신을 최대한 피력할 수 있도록 하는 답변이 좋다.

예1) When I worked in the hotel, I heard that I have to learn how to rest. They told me that I need to do some other activities for my day off. I think I heard that because I am bit of workaholic. When I was really sick, I couldn't find any other things except work. So I finally realized that I am sort of person who need to know some other things to do rather than work. So these days I am trying to do some exercise when I have some free time. I found that there is so much fun in there. I am getting really like it.

예2) I heard that I am bit too hurry to do some tasks. I know it is big problem. So these days I am having fun to play Chinese chess, it gives me certain time to think about what I have to do next. It also teaches me how important to have a little bit of time to do next task rather than moving without thinking. I am sure all the works are not like Chinese chess, but I am bit different person now because of that I will do the same things in my work.

What key asset can you offer in this job?

여러분이 생각하는 장점과 능력은 무엇이고 이러한 것들이 여러분의 직업을 수행하는데 어떻게 도움이 되고 앞으로 회사에 어떻게 이익을 줄 수 있겠느냐는 질문이다.

예1) My openness to people and work will help the company be better. I love people and my work. I never hesitate to meet new people and to try new work. The most important lesson through my life is when I try to open myself, there is always answer. I know I am just one person, but when I try to do my best to others, they will open their mind and we can work together to make big difference for the better future.

Question about the job and the company(지원한 일과 회사에 관한 것)

자신의 일에 대한 정확한 파악과 회사에 대한 충분한 조사는 인터뷰에 응하는 사람에게는 필수적인 것이다. 지원의 이유와 관심의 정도를 반드시 표현해줄 수 있는 자신의 의견을 반드시 준비하자.

Why did you apply for the position?

자기가 지원하는 회사에 대해서 잘 알고 있는 것은 매우 중요하다. 특히 무엇을 배우게 될 것인지, 그리고 그러한 것들을 통해 회사에 공헌할 수 있을지에 대해서 자신의 의견을 말해줄 수 있어야 한다.

예1) I always want to be a cook. I know I still have to learn a lot more but I have never hesitated to learn to be a better cook. Graduation is just another start and for this new start, I decided to apply for this position which is what I have always dreamed about. I really want to have this chance and I will do my best.

What do you know about our company?

앞서의 질문과 유사하지만 조금 더 큰 질문이 될 수 있다. 단순히 회사에 대한 칭찬이나 상투적인 말보다는 구체적인 자신의 느낌을 말하고 회사를 통해 무엇을 이루고 싶다는 정도로 의견을 말해주면 된다.

예1) I heard that so many things about the company. Especially what I like is how much I can learn through the company. I love to challenge some new tasks and these things make me feel better. The company has operated for many years and it has kept excellent reputation and I want to be a part of them. I will learn much more about cooking with people who are in this company and I will be proud of myself, when I become a member of this company.

Why do you think you are suitable for this job?
Why should we hire you for this position?

모든 질문이 다 중요하지만 이 질문만큼 자신의 논리를 남에게 이해시켜야 하는 중요성이 부각되는 질문도 없다. 반드시 깊은 생각을 바탕으로 자신의 장점과 기술 그리고 성격적인 면들을 부각시켜 대답을 준비하도록 하자.

예1) I heard that when someone does what they like to do there will be always good results. I love to cook and I have always dreamed about being a cook. What I learnt from my college education is not everything about cooking, that' s why I am here. I want to learn more about cooking and I am ready to do it. I believe that through this job I will be not only a better cook but also a happy person who do what he/she likes to do.

Questions about education and experiences
(자신의 교육과 경험에 관한 것들을 묻는 질문)

What was the most impressive thing in your student life so far? What did you learn from your school life?

학교 생활을 통해 여러분이 배운 것은 무엇입니까? 이러한 것들이 우리의 회사와 여러분 자신의 발전에 어떻게 도움을 줄 수 있을까 하는 것을 묻는 질문이다.

예1) I remember many things about my school years, but one thing I don't want to forget is my school friends and what we did together. We did so many things together; I still remember when we work together for cooking contest, sometimes we had to stay all night for the preparation and sometimes we argued for certain matter. If someone say what I learn from my school life I definitely say how great friendship and I want to have more in my career.

Have you experienced working with teams?

다른 사람과 같이 일해본 경험에 대해 준비하는 것은 매우 중요하다. 우리가 일하려고 하는 곳은 사람과 같이 일하는 곳이기 때문이다. 어떻게 다른 사람과 호흡하고 일했느냐가 매우 중요한 요소라는 것은 굳이 강조하지 않아도 알 것이다.

예1) I have two different kinds of team work experience. I used to work with my college mate for cooking competition. That was great and I learnt so many things. Especially I realized that how important to understand others. What I found that every person has different thinking and abilities. Also I learnt that work allocation is very important too.

My the other team work experience was my internship in real industry. What can I say.. That was really great. I met so many experts and I realized that I still had to learn so many things.
So I keep opening my ear and eye for better cook and I will do the same things for future.

How did you choose your major?
How has your education benefited you?
How has your education helped with your current job?
What specific work related coursed have you taken?
What kind of experiences do you have for the job?
Tell us about your qualification.

위의 질문들 역시 인터뷰를 준비하는 학생들이 반드시 준비해야만 하는 것들이다.

Tip

성격을 묘사하는 단어들이다. 반드시 익히자. 단어장에 기록하고 반드시 그 뜻이 의미하는 바를 익히도록 하자.

Personality

Gently / kind / thoughtful / affectionate / responsible / positive / enthusiastic / bright / cheerful / cooperative / sociable / adaptable / friendly / open-minded / patient / quiet / flexible / warm-hearted / honest / responsive / gently / sympathetic / independent / efficient / frank / confidant

02 이력서와 자기소개서 작성

이력서는 서면으로 하는 인터뷰라고 생각하면 될 것 같다. 인터뷰에서 실수하고 싶은 사람은 없을 것이다. 이력서에서의 실수는 인터뷰에서 자신의 소개에 대해 황당한 말을 하는 것과 같은 것이다. 확인하고 또 확인해야 하는 부분이다.

영문이력서 작성은 한글로 작성된 이력서와는 조금은 다르다. 일단 성별과 사진의 첨부는 필요 없다고 보면 된다. 하지만 가끔 사진을 첨부해달라는 경우가 있기는 하다. 사진의 선택은 너무 캐주얼하여 보기 민망할 정도는 안 되고 일반적인 증명사진 정도 그리고 조금은 웃는 모습을 보여주어도 상관없을 것 같다.

자기소개서의 핵심은 자신이 이 직업을 위해 무엇을 해왔는가와 자신의 인생경험을 통해 무엇을 배웠는가이다. 그러한 노력과 경험이 이 직장에 어떻게 도움이 되고 어떻게 회사에 이익이 되는지에 대해서 서술하는 것이다. 내용은 명료하고 정확하고 바른 어구를 사용해야 할 것이다. 역시 이력서의 작성에서처럼 어떠한 사소한 실수도 있어서는 안 될 것이다.

이력서 작성시 반드시 들어가야 하는 내용

1) 기본적인 인적 사항

Name (이름) , Address (주소), Contact number (연락처), e mail (이 메일)

2) 기본적인 교육과 경력에 관한 것

Education(교육 경력), Work experience(직장 경험), Skills and capabilities (기술, 능력), Competent in working as a team(팀원으로 일해본 경력), Speak fluently in English, Japanese, and Chinese(언어 능력), Skilled in computer (컴퓨터 활용관련 능력), Food safety and Hygiene certificate(식음료 관련 자격증), First-aid certificate, Clean driving license(기타 자격증), Awards(수상경력), Reference(참고인, 자신의 경력을 증명해주고 자신에 대해 평가해줄 수 있는 사람에 대한 연락처, 간단한 신상명세).

영문이력서 작성의 예)

PERSONAL DETAILS(인적 사항)

Residential Address :

Mobile :

Date of Birth :

Nationality :

Business Attire with smile Passport size of photo Hair pulled away Head shot only

사진

CAREER OBJECTIVES(목표)

A career objectives targeted to internship for which you are applying. An xxx position in an organization(or in an organization seeking xxx and xxx)

Ex) My ambition is to gain challenging work experience in the Tourism Industry where I can be a part of the success of a dynamic and innovative organization.

EDUCATION HISTORY(교육)

In reverse chronological order(most recent qualification first to high school qualification last. Do not need to include primary school)

Month Year–Month Year Full name of Education Institution, Town, Country

Certificate/Diploma/Bachelor Degree/Master…

Expected graduation : Month/Year

Month Year–Month Year Full Name High School, Town, Country

Pls include major or subject (if it related to your internship objectives)

WORK EXPERIEINCE(직장)

In reverse chronological order

Highest most relevant experience internship for which your are applying.

Month Year–Month Year Company, Town, Country

Name of position held–Occupational status

(Casual/Par–time/full time)

Responsibilities and Achievement

Use power verb starts to clearly outline actual duties

Highlight achievements with percentage or figures where possible Include participation in conference and seminar

OTHER SKILLS AND CERTIFICATES(자격증)

Computing skills

Language skiils

Other ;

KEY SKILLS(인간관계관련 기술)

Performance focused competencies that relate to those required in the type of internship you are applying for

- Communication

  Conducted hour-long guided tours to groups of more than 40 tourists (Stanford Malls Pty Ltd)

- Teamwork

  Worked as part of the marketing team to develop and implement a number of marketing initiatives (Phoenix Foundation Inc)

- Leadership

  Supervised and motivated a team of 10 employees (See Melbourne Tours)

- Problem Solving

  Stationed at the Customer Service Desk, act as the source of information to answer all customer queries relating to retail store locations and Stanford Malls Gift Certificates (Stanford Malls Pty Ltd)

INTEREST AND ACTIVITIES(흥미, 취미활동)

Include performance that demonstrate a community/team work involvement or individual dedication or a special interest

REFEREES(참고인)

Provide 2-3 professional referees (persons). Don't forget to contact you referees to participate them should they be contacted.

자기소개서 작성시 반드시 들어가야 하는 내용

날짜, 자신의 주소, 지원하는 회사의 주소, 담당자(이름을 알고 있는 경우 표기하고 모르는 경우 직책을 대신해서 씀), 지원하는 포지션(처음 인사 (Dear라고 시작하는 부분)과 주소 사이에 반드시 넣어준다), 인사(영어로 Dear라고 시작하는 부분), 경력에 관한 내용, 인생관에 관한 내용, 인터뷰에 응하고 싶다는 내용, 그리고 구체적인 연락처, 마무리 인사(Yours Sincerely라고 적는 부분), 자신의 서명(마무리 인사와 자신의 이름 사이에 친필로 적음), 자신의 이름(워드 프로세서로 작성)으로 구성한다.

예 1)

Sarah Student
20 Marina St,
Milton 4064
Student 1@example.com.au

Friday 1st June 2007

Mr Edward Long
Recruitment Manager
Hilton Hotel
2014 King Street,
Melbourne VIC 3000

Re : Application for position of Tour Guide

Dear Mr Long,

My unique mix of previous work experience and my status as a student of the University of New South Wales makes me an ideal Candidate for the above position. I am keen to join Hilton Melbourne and to be a part of the team responsible for showcasing Melbourne to the International market.

As I approach the end of my 4th year in a Bachelor of Tourism (Marketing and Hospitality Management), I am eager to put into practice the knowledge I have acquired over the course of my degree. With a credit average in my Tourism and Marketing subjects, I have a strong foundation of knowledge in these areas.

My 3 years experience within Tourism has fostered my interest and understanding of this dynamic industry. As a part of the See Melbourne Tours Team, I worked in all areas of operation for this leading tourist attraction. I was later promoted to the role of Relief Supervisor – testimony to my dedication and performance. From there I joined my current employer, Stanford Malls, where I worked as a tour guide in Sydney Centre. In addition to my Tourism Industry experience, I have also worked as a Volunteer Marketing Assistant for Phoenix Foundation, a non-profit organization. I have since decided that an amalgamation of these two industries – tourism and marketing – is the career path that I am set to explore.

Finally, I know that this opportunity within Hilton Melbourne Tours Team would be mutually beneficial. I am a highly motivated and reliable individual who works well as part of a team. I look forward to discussing this opportunity with you further. My resume is provided for your reference on the the following pages. Please feel free to contact me at anytime to arrange an interview: (M) 0401 044 558 or (H) 92355 5455

Thank you for your time and consideration.

Yours truly,

Sarah Student

예 2)

Cover Letter

15.03.2011
Manager of Lotte Hotel
#201 Suesomun Gu
Seoul , Korea

RE : PR officer.

Dear Recruit Manager :

As a second year at Han Yang University in Seoul, I am interested in working as a PR officer, the position you offered in the classified as in Chosun Daily Newspaper dated 20. Feb. 2011.

I have enclosed my resume, showing that my one-year experience in the United States. Two years ago, I attended classes at UCLA, as a full time student. That experience has, not only improved my ability in communications in English, but also given me an excellent opportunity to learn about the importance of respecting customers and ways of thinking that are inherently different among various kinds of people. I can make use of my English skills and my ability to put myself in offering the customers the best service.

I would appreciate if I can have an interview with you. / I feel that I can offer my experience and your company can gainfully employ me in the front line as a PR personnel or its equivalent./ I hope that you will consider my application and I look forward to meeting you for an interview.

Sincerely Yours

Cul-su Kim

불규칙 동사표

원형	과거형	과거분사형(pp)	원형	과거형	과거분사형(pp)
be	was, were	been	lend	lent	lent
bear	bore	born	make	made	made
break	broke	broken	pay	paid	paid
bring	brough	tbrought	put	put	put
build	built	built	read	read	read
buy	bought	bought	say	said	said
catch	caught	caught	see	saw	seen
choose	chose	chosen	send	sent	sent
cut	cut	cut	sing	sang	sung
do	did	done	speak	spoke	spoken
draw	drew	drawn	steal	stole	stolen
eat	ate	eaten	take	took	taken
find	found	found	teach	taught	taught
give	gave	given	tell	told	told
hold	held	held	think	thought	thought
hurt	hurt	hurt	throw	threw	thrown
keep	kept	kep	tunderstand	understood	understood
know	knew	known	write	wrote	written

비교급

원급	비교급	최상급
old	older	oldest
young	younger	youngest
fast	faster	fastest
nice	nicer	nicest
wise	wiser	wisest
large	larger	largest
pretty	prettier	prettiest
happy	happier	happiest
easy	easier	easiest
big	bigger	biggest
hot	hotter	hottest
thin	thinner	thinnest
famous	more famous	most famous
handsome	more handsome	most handsome
important	more important	most important
good/well	better	best
many/much	more	most
little	less	least

Part 1. SERVICE ENGLISH

해설

1. Greeting & Introduce(인사 및 자기소개)

Dialogue 1

A: 안녕하세요, 저는 Jack이라고 합니다.
B: 안녕하세요. 저는 Jill입니다.
A: 만나서 반갑습니다.
B: 저도 만나서 반갑습니다.
A: 오늘은 어떠세요?
B: 매우 좋습니다.
A: 만나서 반가웠습니다.
B: 저도요. 다음에 뵙죠.
A: 네 다음에 뵙겠습니다.

Dialogue 2

A: 반갑습니다. 고객님! 힐튼호텔에 오신 것을 환영합니다. 오늘은 어떠신지요?
B: 매우 좋습니다. 고맙습니다. 당신은 어떠신지요?
A: 그렇습니다. 서울에서 무엇을 하실 계획이신지요?
B: 지금 쇼핑하려고 합니다.
A: 좋으시겠습니다.
좋은 시간 되세요.

Dialogue 3

A: 오늘 어떻게 보내시고 계시는지요?
B: 오늘 계속 바쁘네요.
A: 무엇을 하시는지요?
B: 인터뷰 준비하고 있습니다.

Dialogue 4

A: Jack, 안녕하세요.
B: 반가워요 Jill.
한동안 뵙지 못했던 것 같습니다. 어떻게 지내세요.
A: 특별한건 없었습니다. Jill은요?
B: 저도 잘 지냅니다.
A: 가족들한테 안부 전해 주세요.
B: 그러지요. 다음에 또 뵐게요.

Dialogue 5

A: 머무시는 동안 불편함은 없으셨는지요?
B: 매우 좋았습니다. 고마워요.
A: 언제 떠나게 되시죠?
B: 비행기가 오후 2시에 떠나게 됩니다.
A: 그렇군요. 티켓은 예약을 확인하셨는지요?
B: 그럼요, 일주일전에 했습니다.
A: 그렇군요. 서울에 다시 한 번 오시기를 바라겠습니다.
B: 저도 그러고 싶어요. 친질하게 대해줘서 고맙습니다.
A: 천만에요. 안전하게 돌아가세요.

2. Requests and Responses(요청과 승낙, 감사, 거절)

Dialogue 1

A: 부탁 좀 들어 줄 수 있겠어요?
B: 어떻게 도와줄까요?
A: 이 커피 필터 청소해 줄래요?
B: 그렇게 할게요.
A: 도와줘서 너무 고마워요.
B: 천만에요.

Dialogue 2

A: 여기 라커룸이 어디 있는지 알려주실 수 있을까요?
B: 제가 안내할게요. 이쪽으로 오세요.
A: 정말 감사합니다.
B: 천만에요.

Dialogue 3

A: 아까 주문서 넣은 것 바꿀 수 없을까요?
B: 미안한데요. 그렇게 하기 힘들 것 같아요. 최소한 10분 전에는 알려줘야만 해요.
A: 알아요, 하지만 손님이 지금 갑자기 마음을 바꾸었다고 해서요.
B: 미안해요. 우리도 어쩔 수 없어요. 다시 주문서를 넣어 주세요.
A: 그럴게요.
B: 정말 미안해요. 그리고 손님한테 음식은 10분 정도 걸린다고 말해주세요.

🕮 Dialogue 4

A: 여보세요. 미스터 Jun씨와 통화할 수 있을까요?
B: 네, 잠시만 기다려 주세요.
C: 예 Jun입니다. 전화 거신 분은 누구시죠?
A: 안녕하세요. 저는 Green이라고 합니다. 지난 주 저녁식사에서 너무 감사했다고 전해드리고 싶어 전화했습니다.
C: 무슨 말씀을요. 즐거우셨다니 매우 기쁩니다. 다음에 오실 기회가 있으시면 언제든 연락주세요.
A: 그럴게요, 너무 감사해요. 다음에 또 통화하지요.

🕮 Dialogue 5

A: 안녕하세요! 고객님 어떻게 도와드릴까요?
B: 화장실이 고장 난 것 같아요.
A: 불편을 끼쳐 드려 정말 죄송합니다. 바로 사람을 올려 보내 드리겠습니다.
B: 부탁드립니다.

🕮 Dialogue 6

A: 펜 좀 쓸 수 있을까요?
B: 네 여기 있습니다.
A: 어디에 서명하면 되죠?
B: 여기 고객 등록카드에 하시면 됩니다.
A: 아 그렇군요. 고마워요.

🕮 Dialogue 7

A: 오늘 점심 같이 할까요?
B: 오늘 한시에 미팅이 있어서 힘들 것 같아요.
A: 그럼 다음에 시간을 한번 마련해 보지요.

🕮 Dialogue 8

A: 저녁은 즐거우셨는지요?
B: 매우 좋았습니다. 고맙습니다.
A: 와인 조금 더 드시겠습니까?
B: 그러지요.
A: 죄송합니다. 와인을 조금 쏟았습니다.
B: 괜찮아요. 테이블에 흘렸는데요 뭐
A: 다른 와인 한잔을 가지고 오겠습니다.
B: 고맙습니다.
A: 금방 돌아오도록 하겠습니다.

3. Making an appointment(약속)

Dialogue 1

A: 컨퍼런스가 시작되려면 시간이 얼마나 남았지?
B: 2시간 밖에 남지 않았습니다.
A: 자 이제 서둘러 주세요.
B: 제가 하던 것을 끝내놓고 바로 Jacky를 도와주겠습니다.
여기 준비하는데 20분 정도 걸릴 것 같습니다. 이것을 끝내고 바로 도와주겠습니다.
A: 좋습니다. 서둘러 주세요. 컨퍼런스가 곧 시작됩니다.

Dialogue 2

A: 일정표 체크해 봤어요?
B: 아직 못했는데, 어땠는데?
A: 이번 주 토요일에 일해야 할 것 같아.
B: 안됐다.. 나도 체크해 봐야 하겠군.
A: 이번 주 토요일에는 정말 바쁘디나봐
B: 그럼 준비 단난히 해야 하겠는데.

Dialogue 3

A: 오늘 무슨 안건을 토의하게 되지?
B: 내일 행사를 위한 준비를 해야 한다고 들었습니다.
A: 아마 그거 필요 없을 거야, 행사가 취소됐다고 들었거든.
B: 아니에요, 새로운 행사가 진행된나고 들었어요,

A: 뭐야, 그럼 내일 우리가 행사를 3가지나 치러야 한다는 이야기잖아.
B: 그래도 조용한 날 보다 바쁜 날들이 난 더 좋더라고요.
A: 나도 그래, 난 그냥 무슨 일이 변경되거나 새로 생기면 최소 2일 정도만 일찍 알 수 있었으면 좋겠어.

Dialogue 4

A: 미스터 김 안녕하세요. 어떻게 도와드릴까요?
B: 오늘 저녁에 예약을 확인하려고 전화했습니다.
A: 7시 30분에 한식당 수라에서의 예약 맞으시지요?
B: 그렇습니다.
A: 예약은 잘되어있습니다. 조금 있으면 오시겠군요.
B: 예약 확인 고맙습니다.
A: 천만에요.

Dialogue 5

A: Jim 오늘 저녁에 뭐할 생각이야?
B: 특별한건 없어.
A: 저녁같이 먹자, 오늘 시간 어때?
B: 그런데 오늘 저녁에 숙제 하나를 끝내긴 해야해.
A: 그럼 내일은?
B: 괜찮아, 어디서 몇 시에 볼까?
A: 내 사무실근처의 바에서 7시에 보면 어떨까?
B: 좋아, 거기에 보자, 안녕

4. Telephone(전화)

Dialogue 1

A: 여보세요.
B: 여보세요. John과 통화할 수 있을까요?
A: 실례하지만 전화 거신 분은 누구시죠?
B: 친구 Tim이라고 하는데요.
A: 잠시만 기다려 주세요.
C: John입니다.
B: John 잘 있었어?
C: 난 잘 있었어, 너는?
B: 나도. 오늘 저녁에 뭐할 거니? 오늘 한가하면 우리집에 바비큐 파티에 올 수 있겠니?
C: 야 재미있겠는데.
B: 내가 언제 태우러 가면 될까?
C: 5시 반 어때?
B: 그럼 이따 보지, 바이

Dialogue 2

A: 반갑습니다. 고객님 J&L 호텔입니다. 어떻게 도와드릴까요?
B: 예약을 하고 싶은데요.
A: 얼마나 오래 머무를 계획이신가요?
B: 2박을 하려고 합니다.
A: 언제 오실려고 하지요?
B: 12월 15일에서 16일까지요.
A: 싱글베드로 하시겠습니까 아니면 더블베드로 하시겠습니까?
B: 더블베드로 하겠습니다.

A: 제가 체크해 드리겠습니다. 잠시만 기다려 주세요.
15일부터 16일까지 더블룸을 예약하실 수 있습니다.
B: 잘됐네요, 그리고 바다가 보이는 방으로 예약을 부탁드려도 될까요?
A: 그럼요, 그렇게 해드리겠습니다.

Dialogue 3

A: 하얏트호텔인가요? 오늘밤에 금연실로 예약이 가능할까요?
B: 네 고객님, 오늘 예약이 가능하십니다. 성함을 알려주시겠습니까?
A: Andrew Chang이라고 합니다.
B: 전화번호 부탁드립니다.
A: 제 전화번호는 555 3452입니다.
B: 다른 것 더 도와드릴 것은 없을까요?
A: 아니요, 고맙습니다.
B: 예약해 주셔서 감사합니다. 오늘 저녁에 뵙겠습니다.

Dialogue 4

A: 여보세요, 저는 제니퍼라고 하는데요, Mr Kim과 통화할 수 있을까요?
B: 죄송하지만 지금 다른 전화를 받고 계시는데요, 메모 남겨 드릴까요?
A: 그럼 될 수 있는 한 빨리 전화연락 부탁드린다고 전해 주세요.
B: 그렇게 하겠습니다. 전화번호주세요.
A: 아마 내 번호를 알고 있을 겁니다.
B: 통화 마치시는 데로 전화 하셨다고 연락드리겠습니다.
A: 고맙습니다.

📖 Dialogue 5

A: Suzy 안녕. 나 Tom이야. 잘 지냈니?

B: Tom 반가워, 오늘 몸이 좋지 않네. 감기 걸려서 하루 종일 집에 있었어.

A: 괜찮은거니? 오늘 하루 종일 전화연락하려고 했었거든 전화가 되지 않더라.

B: 배터리가 다 되었나봐.

A: 몸 잘 돌봐야 할 것 같구나. 저녁에 다시 전화할게.

B: 전화 줘서 고맙다. 안녕

5. Travel(여행)

Dialogue 1

A: 일본에 일주일 가려고 하는데요. 어디를 어떻게 가야 할까 고민입니다.
B: 패키지 투어로 가시겠습니까 아니면 개별여행을 선호하시나요?
A: 실례하지만 전화 거신 분은 누구시죠?
B: 패키지 투어를 생각해본 적은 있는데요.
A: 코리아 여행사의 상품을 추천하고 싶습니다. 전화하셔서 언제 가려고 한다고 말씀하시면 여행상품에 대해서 자세히 안내해 줄 겁니다.
B: 고마워요. 전화번호가 어떻게 되죠?
A: 4430-8891번입니다.

Dialogue 2

A: 여보세요. 코리아 여행사죠? 일본으로 가는 투어에 대해서 알아보려고 전화했습니다.
B: 일본 어디에 가려고 하시는지요. 그리고 기간은 어느 정도를 예상하는지요?
A: 오월의 첫 번째 주에 도쿄에 가려고 합니다.
B: 그러시다면 5월 1일에 출발하는 비행기를 예약하겠습니다. 그리고 거기에서 4일 동안 도쿄에 머무르시면서 유명한 관광지를 구경하시게 됩니다.
A: 비용은 얼마나 하지요?
B: 여행하시는 한분에 800불 정도 소요됩니다.
A: 그 비용에 무엇이 포함되어 있는 것인가요?
B: 비행기 표와 숙박비 그리고 매일의 식사 3끼가 포함됩니다.
A: 나한테 맞는 상품인 것 같군요. 예약을 해주시겠습니까?

📖 Dialogue 3

A: 좋은 아침입니다. (안녕하세요)
B: 안녕하세요, 어떻게 도와드릴까요?
A: 이번 4월에 뉴욕에서 있을 관광학회에 참석하려고 하는데요.
B: 호텔예약과 교통편을 알아봐 드릴 수 있을 것 같군요.
동행하시는 분이 있으신지요?
A: 아니요. 그리고 텍사스에 가서 지역 여행자 협회에서 미팅을 가져야 합니다.
B: 먼저 대한 항공을 타시고 서울에서 뉴욕까지 11시간 비행하시게 되고요, 저녁에 도착하시게 되겠군요. 그리고 다음비행기는 선생님 스케줄에 맞추어 조정해 놓겠습니다.
A: 고맙습니다.
B: 무슨 말씀을요, 언제든지 부탁해 주세요.

📖 Dialogue 4

A: 안녕하세요, 어떻게 도와드릴까요?
B: 3월 2일에 파리로 가는 비행기를 예약하고 싶은데요.
A: 잠시만 기다려주세요. 제가 비행 스케줄을 체크해 보겠습니다.
B: 네.
A: 정말 죄송합니다. 고객님. 3월 2일에는 비행기 좌석이 힘들것 같습니다.
그렇지만 3월 2일에는 가능할 것 같습니다.
B: 물론입니다. 편도로 예약할까요? 왕복으로 예약할까요?
A: 왕복으로 부탁드립니다.
B: 그렇게 해드리겠습니다. 여행하시는 당일 여권 챙기시는것 잊지 마시구요.
A: 그렇게 할게요.

6. Airport(공항)

Dialogue 1

A: 여권과 티켓을 보여주시겠습니까?
B: 여기 있습니다.
A: 복도좌석을 하시겠습니까 아니면 창가좌석을 드릴까요?
B: 복도좌석을 부탁합니다.
A: 짐을 몇 개를 가지고 계시는지요?
B: 두 개있습니다.
A: 짐들을 여기에 놓아 주시겠습니까?
B: 네
A: 여기 보딩패스가 있습니다. 55번 개찰구에서 탑승하시면 됩니다. 그리고 출발시간은 7시 50분입니다.
B: 고맙습니다.

Dialogue 2

A: 반갑습니다. 어떻게 도와드릴까요?
B: 파리로 가는 비행기 시간을 체크해 보고 싶습니다.
A: 죄송합니다. 고객님, 비행기가 30분 정도 지연되고 있습니다.
B: 정말요! 무슨 일이죠?
A: 뉴욕국제공항의 날씨가 매우 좋지 않아 그런 것으로 알고 있습니다. 탑승구에서 기다려 주셔야 할 것 같습니다. 불편을 끼쳐 드려 대단히 죄송합니다.
B: 어쩔 수 없을 것 같네요. 방송 나올 때까지 기다릴게요.
A: 다시 한 번 불편을 끼쳐 죄송하다는 말씀드리고 싶습니다.

Dialogue 3

A: 5월 5일에 파리로 가는 저의 비행기 스케줄을 취소하고 다른 날로 조정했으면 좋겠는데요.

B: 잠시만 기다려 주세요. 제가 체크해 드리겠습니다.

A: 좌석은 충분하게 남아있을까요?

B: 그런 것 같지는 않습니다만 언제로 비행기 스케줄을 바꾸시고 싶으신지요?

A: 5월 6일로 바꾸려고 합니다만

B: 죄송합니다만 그날에는 비행기에 여분의 좌석이 없습니다. 그 다음날에는 가능하구요.

A: 그럼 다음날 아침에 예약을 부탁해도 될까요?

B: 9시 15분 비행기는 어떠시겠습니까?

A: 그렇게 해 주세요.

Dialogue 4

A: 미국에는 얼마나 머무를 계획이신지요?

B: 6일 동안 머무를 예정입니다.

A: 미국에는 처음방문하시는 건가요?

B: 아니요, 일전에 몇 번 방문한 적이 있습니나.

A: 직업이 무엇이신지요?

B: 저는 과학자입니다.

A: 어디에서 머무르게 되시는 지요?

B: 뉴욕에 있는 프라자 호텔에서 머무르게 됩니다.

A: 미국을 방문하시는 목적은 무엇이신지요?

B: 사업차 왔습니다. 과학박람회에 참석하게 됩니다.

A: 그렇군요. 즐거운 여행되시고요. 고맙습니다.

Dialogue 5

A: 세관에 신고하실 물건은 있으신지요?
B: 네 한 가지 있습니다. 한국술 한 병이 있습니다. 미국에 있는 친구를 위한 건데요.
A: 그 술의 가격은 얼마나 되지요?
B: 한 20불 정도 될 겁니다.
A: 다른 건 있을까요?
B: 그게 다예요
A: 즐거운 하루 보내세요.

Dialogue 6

A: 이 신고서를 작성해야만 하나요?
B: I-94 신고서를 작성해야 합니다.
A: 다 적성하면 어떻게 해야 하지요?
B: 도착하시고 난 후 출입국심사원에게 제출하셔야 합니다.
A: 출입국심사대를 통과하면 어떻게 해야 하지요?
B: 수화물 창구에 가셔서 짐을 찾으신 후 세관을 통과하시면 됩니다.
A: 도움 주셔서 감사합니다.
B: 천만에요.

7. In the airplane(비행기 안)

📖 Boarding

S: 탑승을 환영합니다. 좌석표를 보여주시겠습니까?
P: 여기 있습니다. 제 좌석은 어디입니까?
S: 40B 복도쪽 좌석입니다. 이쪽으로 오세요. 제가 안내해드리겠습니다.
P: 고맙습니다.
S: 손님의 짐은 위쪽 선반에 넣어두세요. 제가 도와드리겠습니다.
P: 알겠습니다.
S: 만약에 도움이 필요하시다면 언제든 불러주십시오.

📖 Take-off

S: 실례합니다, 손님. 저희 비행기는 곧 이륙할 것입니다. 손님의 좌석을 앞으로 당겨주시기 바랍니다.
P: 서울에서 로스엔젤레스까지 비행시간이 어떻게 되시요?
S: 날씨상황에 따리 조금 다르지만 보통은 10시간이 소요됩니다.
P: 일겠습니다.
S: 기장이 좌석벨트 표시등을 끌 때까지 좌석벨트를 매고 앉아있으시기 바랍니다.
P: 잘 알겠습니다.

In-flight service

S: 저녁으로 소고기와 돼지고기 중 어떤 것으로 드시겠습니까?
P: 소고기로 주세요. 어쨌든 메뉴를 좀 보여주실 수 있나요?
S: 메뉴는 손님 앞의 좌석주머니에 있습니다. 음료 드시겠습니까?
P: 맥주주세요.
S: 어떤 종류를 맥주를 원하십니까?
P: 하이트있나요?
S: 네, 여기 맥주 있습니다.
다른 것 더 필요하신가요? 식사 맛있게 하십시오.

In-flight movie

P: 도착시간이 언제인가요?
S: 파리시각으로 저녁 8시에 도착합니다.
P: 알겠습니다.
오늘 기내 영화는 어떤 것을 상영하는지요?
S: 코메디입니다. 프로그램에 대한 정보는 기내잡지 안에 수록되어 있습니다.
P: 영화는 언제 보여주는가요?
S: 식사서비스 후에 보여드립니다.
P: 만약 가능하다면 좌석을 바꾸어도 되는가요?
S: 물론입니다. 제가 빈좌석이 있는지를 알아보겠습니다.

🕮 Handling problems

S: 승무원호출등이 켜졌네요. 무엇을 도와드릴까요?
P: 네, 지금 몸이 안 좋은 것 같아요.
S: 어디가 안 좋으십니까?
P: 두통이 심합니다. 아스피린 있으세요?
S: 물론입니다. 그것 외에 다른 것도 필요하십니까?
P: 괜찮아요.
S: 혹시나 해서 담요와 따뜻한 물을 가져다 드리겠습니다.
P: 정말 고맙습니다.

🕮 Attending passengers

P: 저녁 식사 전에 잠시 잠을 잘까합니다.
S: 머리 위 선반에서 베개와 담요를 꺼내드리겠습니다. 손님, 저녁메뉴 주문을 받고 있습니다. 닭고기와 소고기 중 어떤 것을 원하십니까?
P: 소고기 주세요. 그러나 내 친구는 지금 자고 있으니 나중에 다시 올 수 있나요?
S: 물론입니다.

🕮 Before landing

S: 실례합니다. 저희 비행기 곧 착륙할 여정입니다. 좌석벨트를 매시고 소지품은 좌석아래에 두시기 바랍니다.
P: 알겠습니다.
S: 오늘 비행은 즐거웠습니까?
P: 아주 좋았습니다. 고맙습니다.
S: 천만에요. 손님을 기내에서 다시 만나 뵙게 되기를 바랍니다.

8. Hotel(호텔)

🕮 Checking-in with reservation

A: 안녕하세요. 힐탑호텔에 오신 것을 환영합니다.
B: 안녕하세요. 싱글 객실이 있는가요?
A: 예약을 하셨습니까?
B: 네, 마이크라는 이름으로 예약을 했습니다.
A: Mr. 마이크, 잠시만 기다려주십시오. 제가 알아보겠습니다.
Mr. 마이크, 5월 27일과 28일까지 싱글 객실 예약이 되어있네요. 숙박계를 작성해주시겠습니까?

🕮 Checking-in without reservation

A: 안녕하세요. 오늘밤 더블 객실이 있나요?
B: 잠시만 기다려주십시오. 알아봐 드리겠습니다. 죄송하지만 저희 호텔은 지금 더블 객실이 없고, 5개의 싱글 객실과 2개의 트윈 객실만이 남아있습니다.
A: 그러면 트윈 객실을 주세요.
B: 알겠습니다. 성함이 어떻게 되십니까?
A: 해리 김입니다.
B: 손님, 얼마동안 여기서 머무를 예정입니까?
A: 이틀 밤 동안입니다. 방값은 어떻게 됩니까?
B: 방값은 여기 객실 가격표에 적혀있습니다.
A: 알겠습니다.
B: 숙박계를 작성해주시겠습니까?
A: 여기 있습니다.
B: 저희 호텔에서 머무르시는 동안 즐거운 시간되시기를 바랍니다.

🕮 Doorman service

A: 안녕하세요? 손님 짐을 도와드릴까요?

B: 네. 여기 있습니다.

A: 짐을 여기에 두시면 제가 가져다 드리겠습니다, 손님. 프런트 데스크로 오십시오.

B: 고맙습니다.

A: 천만에요. 즐거운 시간 보내십시오.

🕮 Doorman service

A: 안녕하세요? 메리어트호텔에 오신 것을 환영합니다.
짐을 도와드릴까요?

B: 괜찮습니다. 별로 무겁지 않아요. 내가 들고 가겠습니다.
어디에서 숙박계를 작성하나요?

A: 프런트데스크는 손님 오른편에 있습니다. 쉽게 찾으실 수 있습니다.

B: 고맙습니다.

A: 천만에요.

🕮 Bellman service

A: 손님 객실로 안내해드리겠습니다.

B: 고맙습니다.

A: 여기는 7층이고 객실은 705호입니다.

B: 방이 아주 좋군요.

A: 손님께서 좋아하시니 저도 기쁩니다.
욕실은 이쪽이고 옷장은 저쪽입니다, 손님.

B: 생수와 맥주가 있나요?

A: 음료는 객실 내의 미니바에서 드실 수 있습니다. 미니바에는 알콜음료, 맥주, 소프트드링크가 구비되어 있습니다.
B: 잘 알겠습니다.
A: 그것 외에 또 다른 것이 필요하십니까, 손님?
B: 그것뿐입니다.
A: 도움이 필요하시면 언제든 불러주십시오.
B: 그렇게 하겠습니다. 도와주셔서 고맙습니다.

Bellman service

A: 한식당이 어디인가요?
B: 지하에 수라 한식당이 있습니다. 가격은 적당합니다.
A: 정말인가요? 그 곳은 언제까지 문을 열고 있나요?
B: 자정까지 문을 열고 있습니다.
A: 그 곳은 예약이 필요한가요?
B: 예약을 하는 것이 더 좋을 듯합니다. 손님을 위해 예약을 해 드릴까요? 몇 시로 해드릴까요?
A: 저녁 7시로 부탁합니다.
B: 예약을 해드리겠습니다.

Communications

A: 안녕하세요. 무엇을 도와드릴까요?
B: 저는 506호에 투숙 중인 테드 베이커입니다. 저 앞으로 온 메시지가 있나요?
A: 잠시만 기다려 주십시오.
네, 메시지가 있습니다. Mr. 마이크가 통화하기를 원하십니다.
B: 오후 4시에 호텔에서 그분을 만나기로 했었는데, 얼마동안 기다렸나요?
A: 대략 30분 정도입니다.
B: 오! 내가 깜박했네요. 당장 그분한테 전화해서 사과를 해야겠네요.

Communications

A: 안녕하세요, 하얏트호텔입니다. 무엇을 도와드릴까요?
B: 레스토랑에서 점심은 언제 제공됩니까?
A: 12시 정각부터입니다. 두 개의 레스토랑에서 12시부터 2시 30분까지입니다.
B: 레스토랑이 어디에 있습니까?
A: 하나는 1층에 위치하고, 나머지 하나는 2층에 위치합니다.
B: 룸서비스도 가능한가요?
A: 물론입니다. 룸서비스는 24시간 가능합니다. 손님 객실에서 언제든 전화할 수 있습니다.
B: 정보를 알려주셔서 감사합니다.

Concierge

A: 관광정보에 관해서 자료를 얻을 수 있을까요?
B: 물론입니다. 무엇을 도와드릴까요?
A: 서울에서 시내관광을 하고 싶습니다. 나에게 좋은 장소를 추천해 주실 수 있나요?
B: 우리 호텔 앞에서 셔틀버스가 운행이 됩니다. 그 버스는 서울의 주요한 관광명소들을 돌고 있습니다. 그 버스는 아침 10시에 출발하며, 매 2시간마다 운행이 됩니다.
A: 그런가요? 내가 버스표를 사야 되는가요?
B: 아닙니다, 그러실 필요가 없습니다. 호텔 투숙객들은 무료입니다.
일행이 몇 명인지만 확약해주십시오.
A: 3명입니다.
B: 좋습니다. 내일 아침에 뵙겠습니다.

Concierge

A: 공항으로 가는 최선의 방법은 무엇인가요?
B: 제 생각으로는 지하철을 타는 것이 좋을 듯합니다.
A: 제일 가까운 지하철역은 어디에 있나요?
B: 호텔 바로 앞에 있습니다.
A: 지하철로는 얼마나 걸리나요?
B: 보통 약 40분 정도 소요됩니다.
A: 잘 알겠습니다. 택시를 타는 것보다 지하철을 타야겠군요.

Operator

A: 안녕하세요, 오퍼레이터입니다. 무엇을 도와드릴까요?
B: Mr. 존스와 통화하고 싶습니다. 저는 브라운인데 회사동료입니다.
A: 잠시만 기다려주십시오. 프런트데스크로 연결해드리겠습니다.
C: 안녕하세요, 프런트데스크입니다. 무엇을 도와드릴까요?
B: Mr. 존스와 통화하고 싶습니다.
C: 성을 다시 한번 말씀해주십시오, 손님.
B: J-O-N-E-S
C: 감사합니다.
끊지 말고 기다려주십시오. 바로 연결해 드리겠습니다.
Mr. 존스 연결되셨습니다.
B: 감사합니다.

🕮 Operator

A: 안녕하세요, 하얏트호텔입니다. 무엇을 도와드릴까요?
B: 저는 829호에 있는 마이크 홍입니다. 내일 아침 7시에 모닝 콜을 부탁드릴게요.
A: 알겠습니다, Mr. 홍. 그 시각에 저희가 모닝 콜을 드리겠습니다.
B: 정말 감사합니다.

🕮 Checking-out

A: 안녕하세요, 호텔 투숙은 어떠신가요?
B: 아주 좋아요. 지금 체크 아웃을 하려합니다.
A: 잠시만 기다려주십시오. 여기 계산서가 있습니다. 미니바에서 무엇을 드셨나요?
B: 생수 한병과 맥주 하나입니다.
A: 최종 계산서는 전부 합하여 310달러입니다, 손님.
B: 계산이 많이 나온 것 같은데요. 세부항목들을 알려주시겠어요?
A: 물론이지요. 150달러는 방값이고, 1-달러는 미니바 사용료, 150달러는 레스토랑식사비이며 세금과 봉사료 포함입니다.
B: 알겠습니다, 신용카드로 계산하겠습니다.
A: 좋습니다. 카드 주시겠습니까?
B: 여기 있습니다.
A: 계산되었습니다. 즐거운 시간 보내셨기를 바랍니다. 저희 호텔에서 다시 뵙게 되기를 바랍니다.

Checking-out

A: 체크아웃하겠습니다. 계산서 좀 주십시오.
B: 물론입니다.
A: 또한 미국달러를 한국 돈으로 환전하고 싶습니다. 오늘 환율은 어떤가요?
B: 환율은 1달러 대 1180원입니다. 얼마정도를 환전하고 싶으신가요?
A: 200달러입니다. 이 정도의 돈으로 한국에서 식사하기에 충분한가요?
B: 어디에서 식사를 하는가에 달려있습니다. 양식을 작성해주시고 여권을 보여주십시오, 손님.
A: 네.
B: 손님 객실 번호와 이름을 말씀해주십시오.

Housekeeping

A: 827호의 톰 존스입니다. 직원을 객실로 올려 보내주실 수 있나요? 내 방의 텔레비전이 작동을 안 합니다.
B: 스위치가 연결되어 있습니까?
A: 네, 확인해보았어요. 얼마 동안 기다려야 하나요?
B: 지금 당장 보내드리겠습니다.
A: 좋아요, 고마워요.

Housekeeping

A: 무엇을 도와드릴까요?
B: 지금 내방 청소를 좀 해주셨으면 합니다.
A: 객실 번호가 어떻게 됩니까?
B: 305호입니다.

A: 룸 메이드를 즉시 올려 보내드리겠습니다.
다른 필요한 것이 있으십니까?
B: 여분의 담요도 필요합니다.
A: 알겠습니다. 여분의 베개와 담요는 객실 내 옷장에 있습니다.
B: 대단히 감사합니다.
A: 천만에요, 손님.

Lost and found service

A: 무엇을 도와드릴까요?
B: 내 생각에 펜을 잃어버린 것 같아요.
A: 어디서 잃어버린지 알고 있으신가요?
B: 확실하지 않은데. 내가 아래층에 있는 레스토랑에서 계산을 할 때 사용을 하였어요.
A: 제가 그곳에서 확인을 해보겠습니다. 또한 분실물 처리소에서도 알아보겠습니다.
B: 부탁드릴께요.
A: 그런 일이 발생되어 죄송합니다. 펜이 발견된다면 연락을 드리겠습니다.

Laundry service

A: 세탁물서비스입니다, 무엇을 도와드릴까요?
B: 셔츠와 바지를 세탁하고 다림질을 부탁할까 합니다.
A: 손님 객실로 직원을 보내겠습니다.
B: 내가 지금 밖으로 나가려고 하는데요.
A: 그러시면 세탁물 수거백에 세탁물들을 넣으시고 객실 문에 걸어주시기 바랍니다.

B: 세탁물 양식서를 작성해야 되나요?
A: 물론입니다, 세탁물은 언제까지 돌려드릴까요?
B: 내일 아침까지 받고싶습니다. 아침 일찍 회의가 있어서요.
A: 우리 호텔은 당일 자정까지 세탁을 해주는 빠른 서비스도 제공하고 있습니다. 물론 추가요금이 발생 합니다.
B: 문제없어요.

9. Restaurant(식당)

Dialogue 1

A: 반갑습니다. 어떻게 도와드릴까요?
B: 일행이 두명인데요.
A: 예약은 하셨는지요?
B: 네 어제 했습니다. 이름은 Lee 라고 합니다.
A: 네 알겠습니다. 예약 확인 되었습니다.
B: 고맙습니다.
A: 제가 테이블로 안내해 드리겠습니다.
B: 혹시 창가 좌석 부탁해도 될까요?
A: 물론입니다. 이쪽으로 오시지요.
B: 고맙습니다.
A: 여기 앉으시죠. 주문하시기 전에 음료 한잔 하시겠습니까?
B: 다이어트 콜라 부탁합니다.
A: 음식을 선택하시고 준비가 되시면 언제든 불러 주세요.
B: 그렇게 하겠습니다.

🕮 Dialogue 2

A: 기다리시는 동안 음료수 한잔 하시겠습니까?
B: 알코올 없는 음료는 있나요?
A: 물론입니다. 각종 주스나 소프트드링크 그리고 커피 티가 있습니다.
B: 다이어트 콜라 두잔 부탁합니다.

🕮 Dialogue 3

A: 주문할 준비가 되셨는지요?
B: 한 일분만 더 주시겠어요? 그런데 오늘 스페셜 메뉴가 뭐지요?
A: 체다 수프가 준비되어 있습니다. 그리고 생선요리와 아스파라거스 그리고 삶은 감자가 준비되어 있습니다.
B: 생선요리는 매운가요?
A: 약간 맵습니다.
B: 그럼 생선 요리로 할게요.
A: 음료는 무엇으로 하시겠습니까?
B: 하우스 와인 한잔 가져다주시겠습니까?
A: 음료 주문하신 것 가지고 금방 돌아오겠습니다.

🕮 Dialogue 4

A: 오늘 메인요리에는 뭐가 있지요?
B: 스테이크, 닭고기, 생선요리, 야채 그리고 감자가 있습니다.
A: 스테이크하고 감자 부탁합니다.
B: 스테이크는 어떻게 해드릴까요?
A: 미디엄 두 웰딘으로 해주세요.

B: 감자는 어떻게 해 드릴까요? 저희는 베이크, 삶은것, 으깬감자, 그리고 튀긴 감자가 있습니다.
A: 베이크드로 해주세요.
B: 셀러드의 드레싱은 어떤 것으로 해 드릴까요?
A: 어떤 종류가 있지요?
B: 이탈리안, 사우젼 아일랜드, 그릭, 프랜치, 오일과 비니거 그리고 저희식당의 하우스 소스가 있습니다.
A: 오일엔 비니거로 하겠습니다.
B: 알겠습니다. 저녁은 한 5분 정도 기다리시면 될 겁니다.

Dialogue 5

A: 식사 마치셨습니까? 식사는 어떠셨는지요?
B: 아주 좋았어요. 특히 양고기가 아주 맛있었어요.
A: 맛있게 하셨다니 좋습니다. 후식 드시겠습니까?
피컨파이가 제공됩니다.
B: 좋아요. 커피도 주시겠습니까?
A: 커피는 어떻게 드릴까요?
B: 커피에 우유를 넣어주세요. 그리고나서 계산서 부탁합니다.

Dialogue 6

A: 닭고기버거 두개와 얼음을 가득채운 코카콜라 주세요.
B: 여기서 드시나요, 가지고 가시나요?
A: 가지고 가겠습니다.
B: 다른 필요한 것 있으신가요? 디저트는 어떤가요?
A: 괜찮아요, 그것으로 충분합니다.

📖 Dialogue 7

A: 음료 무엇으로 하실지 정하셨나요?
B: 알코올이 들어있는 음료는 마시고 싶지 않아요. 음, 혹시 소프트 드링크 있나요?
A: 어떤 종류의 소프트 드링크를 원하시나요?
B: 저는 신선한 망고주스로 할게요.
A: 알겠습니다. 손님은 무엇으로 하시겠습니까?
C: 평상시처럼 맥주로 할게요.
A: 여기 맥주와 주스 있습니다. 맛있게 드십시오.

📖 Dialogue 8

A: 아침 주문하시겠습니까?
B: 아침 뷔페로 할께요.
A: 좋습니다. 음료는 무엇으로 하시겠습니까?
B: 커피주세요.
A: 커피는 어떻게 드릴까요?
B: 블랙 커피로 주세요 (혹은 커피와 설탕, 크림을 빼고)
A: 다른 것 더 필요하십니까? 커피 더 드릴까요?
C: 네, 좋아요.
A: 아침은 어떠셨나요?
B: 정말 좋았어요.
A: 좋으셨다니 저희도 기쁩니다.
B: 계산서 부탁합니다.
A: 물론입니다. 당장 가지고 오겠습니다.

10. Cooking(요리)

Dialogue 1

A: 반갑습니다! 여러분, 오늘 600여 명의 손님을 맞이하게 됩니다. 여러분이 빨리 움직여 주어야 준비가 될 수 있을 것 같습니다. 먼저 David는 스크램블 에그부터 시작해 주시구요.
Kate는 Cold 뷔페 섹션을 체크해주세요. 그리고 준비가 되면 주방에서 음식을 가져가 Cold 뷔페 섹션을 채워주세요.
B&C : 네 그렇게 하겠습니다.

A: 서비스 접시는 다 어디다 두었죠?
B: 바로 거기에 있습니다.
A: David, 메인요리 조리 시작해줄래요? 테이블 14번에서 메인을 조리해달라고 부탁했습니다. 그리고 다시 한 번 확인해 주시구요.
B: 네 그렇게 하겠습니다.
A: 그리고 오늘 스페셜 메뉴는 더 이상 남아 있지 않다고 말해 주세요.
C: 네 그렇게 하겠습니다.

Dialogue 2

A: 뭐 조리하고 있는 거야?
B: 응 생선
A: 내가 도와줄까?
B: 아니야 괜찮아
A: 요리하는 거 좋아하니?
B: 난 요리하는 게 재미있어
A: 디저트도 만들거니?
B: 아직 무얼 만들지 결정 못했어.

A; 사과파이 어때? 나 파이같은거 잘 만들거든.
B: 그럼 사과파이 어떻게 만드는지 알려줄래?
A: 그럴게. 먼저 우유랑, 밀가루 그리고 설탕을 준비하고, 사과를 자르고 준비된 것들을 모두 넣는 거야
B: 냄새가 정말 좋구나. 우리가 만든 생선요리하고 사과파이를 먹자!

Dialogue 3

A: 냄새 좋은데!! 뭐 조리하는 거야?
B: 치즈피자하고 홈메이드 감자튀김 그리고 마늘빵을 만들고 있어
A: 정말 오븐을 어떻게 이용하는지 알기는 아는 거니?
B: 그럼, 먼저 오븐을 켜고 20분 정도 놔두는 거야
A: 훌륭하군, 감자는 다 썰어 놓았어?
B: 물론! 집에서 맛있는 음식 만드는 것 정말 쉽지!

Dialogue 4

A: 한국음식 한 가지 추천해 주실래요?
B: 소고기 좋아하세요.
A: 그럼요
B: 마늘과 양념으로 잘 재운 소갈비가 한국에서 매우 인기가 좋고 특별한 음식이에요
A: 재료로는 무엇이 필요하지요?
B: 간장하구요. 잘게 썬 생강, 갈은 양파와 배, 그리고 다지 마늘이 필요해요. 참기름하고 후추 그리고 가장 중요한 갈비가 필요하지요.
A: 와우! 정말 맛있겠는데요.
B: 좋아하실 거예요

🕮 Dialogue 5

A: 홍차 잘 만드는법 알고 계세요?

B: 기꺼이 가르쳐 드리겠습니다! 첫 번째로 끓는 물 준비하시구요. 차 잎을 넣기 전에 반드시 차 주전자를 뜨거운 물로 데워주세요. 그리고 물은 벼려 주시구요. 그리고 찻잎과 끓는 물을 넣고 약 4분 정도 놔두세요.

A: 레몬 같은 거 넣어도 될까요?

B: 원하시면 넣으셔도 됩니다. 어떤 사람들은 블랙티를 선호하기도 하지요. 그런데 전 밀크티가 더 좋아요.

A: 얼마나 자주 차를 드시죠?

B: 하루에 서너 잔 정도 마시는 것 같아요. 그리고 전 차 향기가 정말 좋답니다.

🕮 Dialogue 6

A: 무엇을 주문하실지 결정하셨나요?

B: 한국에서 인기 있는 음식은 무엇이지요?

A: 무엇을 좋아하시는지에 달렸는데요, 소고기 요리를 좋아하시나요, 아니면 닭고기 요리를 선호하시나요?

B: 소고기, 닭 말고는 다른 건 없나요?

A: 그렇다면 야채요리는 어떠세요? 잡채, 비빔밥 이런 것들이 준비되어 있습니다.

B: 실례하지만 그 요리들에 대해서 좀 설명해주실 수 있으세요.

A: 물론입니다. 잡채는 감자로 만든 국수를 시금치, 버섯, 계란 지단, 당근, 그리고 양파와 함께 볶은 것을 말합니다. 들어가는 재료는 바꾸셔도 되구요.

B: 그럼 채식만을 하는 사람들이 먹을 수 있는 건가요?

A: 그럼요, 소고기 없이 주문하셔도 됩니다.

B: 그럼 비빔밥도 채식만 하는 사람들이 먹을 수 있는 음식인가요?

A: 고기를 빼고 드실 수 있습니다. 비빔밥은 쌀밥과 야채 그리고 고기가 같이 나와 테이블에서 즉석해서 썩어 드실 수 있는 음식입니다. 거기에 매운 양념과 참기름을 넣어 맵게 즐기실 수도 있으세요.

Part 2. GRAMMAR

해답

■ 제1장

1. 명사(고유), 동사(과거형)
2. 대명사(인칭대명사, 주격), 동사(현재형), 명사(보통명사)
3. 부사, 형용사
4. 대명사(인칭대명사, 목적격)
5. 명사(보통)
6. 감탄사
7. 접속사(등위)
8. 전치사

■ 제2장

1. Please don't force me to read this.
2. Simpson was very tired so he made her do all his work.
3. I sometimes had my work done my brother.
4. She married a good looking man.
5. He resembles his father.
6. b
7. b
8. b

■ 제3장

1. a
2. b
3. c
4. …a few days.
5. …well known movie stars…

■ 제4장

1. a
2. b
3. c
4. …ours is too…
5. …and I have something in…
6. … matters is the company…

■ 제5장

1. They met Mr.clark yesterday.
2. My family moved to Seoul three years ago.
3. When did you go to so many cities in Korea?
4. Have you seen Brad and Jennifer recently?
5. Mixes
6. Doesn't clean
7. Do
8. Doesn't
9. 부정문 : They don't make expensive cars in their company.
   의문문 : Do they make expensive cars in their company?
10. He is having a fun…
11. I am not…
12. His grandfather has been ill since last winter.
13. She goes to bed at eleven o'clock every night.
14. I jog in the park every morning.
15. Where are you going now?
16. How are they doing these days?
17. Have worked
18. Haven't eaten

■ 제6장

1. Would
2. May
3. d
4. a
5. must suffered → must be suffered
6. needs to be adapted → needs to adapt

■ 제7장

1. loved
2. built
3. were
4. was making → was made
5. was fed → feed
6. was → were
7. in
8. from
9. in
10. off
11. with
12. The work can be finished by her on time. Can the work be finished….
13. The homework wasn't done by me yesterday. The homework was done by me…
14. The bank was robbed by some men yesterday.
15. The diary has been written for ten years by him.
16. That magazine is sold well in here.

■ 제8장

1. 명사(고유), 동사(과거형)
2. 대명사(인칭대명사, 주격), 동사(현재형), 명사(보통명사)
3. 부사, 형용사
4. 대명사(인칭대명사, 목적격)
5. 명사(보통)
6. 감탄사
7. 접속사(등위)
8. 전치사

■ 제9장

1. not
2. Both
3. Am
4. Whether
5. a
6. b
7. b
8. a
9. c
10. b
11. so → but
12. either → because of
13. which → who
14. was → were
15. whose → who
16. which → where
17. where → when
18. cause → causes

■ 제10장

1. rains
2. drives
3. will order
4. don't
5. will give
6. don't leave
7. snows
8. am
9. come
10. doesn't
11. I give → I will give
12. …if he invites… → if he will invite
13. If you will see.. → If you see
14. You be … → You will be
15. If you will ask.. → If you ask me
16. … if it snows.. → if it will snow tomorrow…
17. If you don't hurry, you will miss the last train.
18. She wants to know whether she can go home or not.
19. If it is true, he must be not guilty.
20. Have learned → had learnt, be much easier → have been easier
21. Had gone → have gone
22. works → work
23. Was → were
24. Go → went

■ 제11장

1. With
2. Since
3. For
4. By
5. With
6. Over
7. To → with, provide food to the poor.
8. Leave from → leave for
9. By supervisor → as supervisor
10. By the telephone → over the telephone

*저|자|소|개

■이 원 화

전) 싱가폴 항공사 승무원
현) 우송대학교 외식산업경영학과 교수

■신 승 훈

전) 호주 쉐라톤 호텔 레스토랑 매니저
현) 영남이공대학 식음료조리계열 교수

PRACTICAL SERVICE ENGLISH 서비스 실무 영어

2011년 8월 31일 초 판 발행
2020년 2월 28일 1판 6쇄 발행

저 자 이원화 · 신승훈
발행인 한 인 환
발행처 도서출판 **기 문 사**
등 록 1978. 8. 9. NO. 6-0637
주 소 서울시 동대문구 안암로 50-1(용두동) 홍신빌딩 3층
전 화 02) 2265-7214/922-8662~8663
팩 스 02) 922-8772

homepage : www.kimoonsa.co.kr
e-mail : book@kimoonsa.co.kr

ISBN : 978-89-7723-509-0 93740

저자와의 협의하에 인지생략

정가 : 15,000원